T0285917

The Soul of Brutes

THE ITALIAN LIST

Carlo Ginzburg

The Soul of Brutes

CALCUTTA LONDON NEW YORK

SERIES EDITOR: ALBERTO TOSCANO

Seagull Books, 2022

ISBN 978 1 803 0 907 2 6

British Library Cataloguing-in-Publication Data
A catalogue record for this book is available from the British Library.

Typeset by Seagull Books Private Limited, Calcutta, India
Printed and bound by Hyam Enterprises, Calcutta, India

These essays, in their diversity,

are a small homage to my friend Naveen Kishore:

to his inventiveness, his energy, his courage.

Contents

Civilization and Barbarism

Civilization, barbarism, and: does 'and' connect or disconnect? Does civilization stand in opposition to barbarism or must we consider the relationship as altogether more complicated? And if so, why?

1. We are used to thinking that the opposition between civilization and barbarism came to us from the Greeks. But a reflection on its ambiguities is also part of the Greek legacy, and its troubling implications still resonate with us.

Here is a story told by Herodotus, 'the father of history' (a long-debated but well-earned title), in the third volume of his *Histories.*[1] It is a digression that is preceded by a detailed list of crimes committed by Cambyses, the Persian king: murder of his brother, incest with his sisters, violating cadavers, defiling the images of the gods. Cambyses, Herodotus concludes, was mad. An example follows:

---

1 *Herodotus*, VOL. 2 [C. 425 BCE] (Alfred Denis Godley trans.) (Cambridge: Harvard University Press, 1982), p. 38.

> I hold it then in every way proved that Cambyses was very mad; else he would never have set himself to deride religion and custom. For if it were proposed to all nations to choose which seemed best of all customs, each, after examinations made, would place its own first; so well is each persuaded that its own are by far the best. It is not therefore to be supposed that any, save a madman, would turn such things to ridicule. I will give this one proof among many from which it may be inferred that all men hold this belief among their customs. When Darius was king, he summoned the Greeks who were with him and asked them what price would persuade them to eat their fathers' dead bodies. They answered that there was no price for which they would do it. Then he summoned those Indians who are called Callatiae, who eat their parents, and asked them (the Greeks being present and understanding by interpretation what was said) what would make them willing to burn their fathers at death. The Indians cried aloud, that he should not speak of so horrid an act. So firmly rooted are these beliefs; and it is, I think, rightly said in Pindar's poem that custom is the queen of all things.[2]

That Darius, king of the Persians, actually attempted such an act appears to be highly unlikely; be that as it may, we will never succeed in reaching certainty on the matter. It is more important to understand the significance of his speech within Herodotus' historical

---

2 *Herodotus*, p. 51.

narration. Pindar's formula, according to which 'custom is the queen of all things'—*nomos ho panton basileus*—would lead us to conclude that all customs are equal, and therefore it is impossible to draw a clear boundary between customs which would be acceptable and those which would not.[3] In other words, our habits seem obvious and natural to us, insofar as they are, like all habits, the result of convention.

And yet, attributing to Herodotus a point of view which we would call radically relativistic would be risky. It is worth remembering a remark by Arnaldo Momigliano: 'Herodotus, one of the founding masters of ethnography, was ready to declare "barbarian" customs superior to the Hellenic ones. But it was a cool, ultimately self-assured, look at foreign civilizations. There was no temptation to yield to them.'[4]

It is the cold look of someone who stages a mental experiment that addresses, on a small scale (but through an extreme example, namely, funeral rites), a more general issue: the variety of human customs. On this point, Darius, the king of Persia, appears as a double, an *alter ego*, of Herodotus. They are both simultaneously the judge and the judged, inside and outside the experiment. When

3 Wilfried Nippel, 'La costruzione dell' "altro"' in Salvatore Settis (ed.), *I Greci: Storia, cultura, arte, società, Volume 1: Noi e i Greci* (Turin: Einaudi, 1996), pp. 165–96; Sally Humphreys, 'Law, Custom and Culture in Herodotus', *Arethusa* 20 (1987): 211–20.

4 Arnaldo Momigliano, 'The Fault of the Greeks' in *Sesto contributo alla storia degli studi classici e del mondo antico*, VOL. 2 (Rome: Ed. di Storia e Letteratura, 1980), pp. 509–24; here, pp. 518–19.

Herodotus says that custom is 'the queen of all things', he simultaneously detaches himself from all things and observes them from afar. We see, looming in the distance, an ongoing dialogue between Herodotus and the sophists who put forward paradoxes like: 'A Cretan says: All Cretans are liars.'[5] Is the Cretan lying or is he telling the truth? What does Herodotus think?[6]

2. The paradox of the Cretan has never ceased to torment logicians: the paradox of Herodotus torments, or should torment, historians and anthropologists. But the unsettling feeling, which we feel in reading the aforementioned passage, that we are facing something contemporary, must be limited by pointing out an element of distance which is linked to the term *nomos*. The translations of 'law' or 'custom' are inevitably inadequate, because the term *nomos* refers to an undifferentiated sphere in which 'right', 'custom' and 'religion' (in the sense in which we use these terms) mingle. *Nomos* is a noun derived from the verb *nemein*: divide (or allocate) according to the law or tradition.[7] We are seemingly back to our starting point, but

---

5 Nippel, 'La costruzione dell' "altro" ', p. 174: '[. . .] there are discussions proposed by the sophists on the relativity of law (*dissoi logoi*) that refer to examples mentioned by Herodotus'. On *dissoi logoi*, see Mario Untersteiner, *I sofisti: testimonianze e frammenti*, VOL. 2 (Milan: Mondadori, 1967), pp. 161–72.

6 Here I pick up some remarks developed in Carlo Ginzburg, 'Lost in Translation: Us and Them', *Hermitage* 2 (2006): 20–2.

7 Émile Benveniste, *Noms d'agent et noms d'action en indo-européen* (Paris: Adrien-Maisonneuve, 1948), p. 79; Émile Benveniste, *Le vocabulaire des institutions indo-européennes*, VOL. 1 (Paris: Minuit, 1969), p. 85; Emmanuel Laroche, *Histoire de la racine nem en grec ancien: nemo, nemesis, nomos, nomizo* (Paris: Klincksieck, 1949).

after having acquired a piece of information: the association between law, custom and division. Even when they look innocent, classifications (and especially dichotomous classifications) have often, although not always, political implications. In a famous passage from his dialogue *The Statesman* [*Politikos*], Plato introduces dichotomous categories into the discussion, aptly beginning with the one which contrasts Greeks and barbarians, through an objection which is formulated by one of the dialogue's interlocutors, named, significantly, the Stranger:

> [. . .] it is very much as if, in undertaking to divide the human race into two parts, one should make the division as most people in this country do; they separate the Hellenic race from all the rest as one, and to all other races, which are countless in number and have no relation in blood or language, they give the single name 'barbarian'; then, because of this single name, they think it is a single species. Or it was as if a man should think he was dividing number into two classes by cutting off a myriad from all the other numbers, with the notion that he was making one separate class, and then should give one name to all the rest, and because of that name should think that this also formed one class distinct from the other. A better division, more truly classified and more equal, would be made by dividing number into odd and even, and the human race into male and female; as for the Lydians and Phrygians and various others, they could be opposed to the rest and split off from them when it was

> impossible to find and separate two parts, each of which formed a class.[8]

3. On this page, Plato rejects the holistic opposition between 'us' and 'them', between Greeks and barbarians, as poorly argued, and therefore untenable. The opposition, and its hierarchical implications, had been reinforced by the wars between the Greeks and Persians. Like Herodotus, although in a different manner, Plato responds to the challenge of the sophists. Today, this term immediately evokes the noun 'sophistry', with its negative connotations—an oblique and distant echo of the negative aura that surrounded the sophists, philosophers who roamed Greece, teaching eloquence. In return for their teaching, the sophists asked for payment: a novelty which created a scandal and cast an enduring shadow on their image. But the theories that the sophists proposed were scandalous as well, because they questioned allegedly self-evident ideas, such as the opposition of Greeks and barbarians—and more generally, the relationship between *nomos* and *physis*, law and habit on the one hand, nature on the other. 'Could what we consider natural be on the contrary the product of convention?' argued the sophists. This is the question that Herodotus asked himself in staging the (presumably fictional) experiment by Darius, the Persian king.

---

8 Plato, *The Statesman* (Harold N. Fowler trans.) (Cambridge: Harvard University Press, 1975[c. 350 BCE]), 262d–263a. See Geoffrey Ernest Richard Lloyd, *Polarity and Analogy: Two Types of Argumentation in Early Greek Thought* (Cambridge: Cambridge University Press, 1966). A reference to this passage can be found also in Anthony Pagden, *The Fall of Natural Man: The American Indian and the Origins of Comparative Ethnology* (Cambridge: Cambridge University Press, 1986), pp. 123–4.

Since a long time, historians of philosophy have dispelled the negative stereotypes that tradition had projected onto the sophists. Today, their questions seem more urgent than ever, even if our answers greatly differ from theirs. Certainly, we must be wary of false continuities, like those tied to language, as in the case of *nomos*/law/habit.

And the Greek term *physis*, which we translate as 'nature', has a different meaning for us than it did for the ancient Greeks. Today, somebody could translate the opposition between *physis* and *nomos*, nature and convention, into a question rife with political implications: 'Do cultural differences have a biological origin?' A translation that would amount to a blatant anachronism. Let us have a quick look at the historical sequence.

4. In his *Statesman*, Plato had opposed the natural dichotomy between men and women to the fictitious divide between Greeks and barbarians. At the beginning of *Politics*, Aristotle cites the distinction between men and women, and the superiority of one over the other, to introduce by way of analogy the distinction between masters and slaves, i.e. between 'natural ruler and natural subject [. . .]. One that can foresee with his mind is naturally ruler and naturally master, and one that can do those things with his body is subject and naturally a slave.' For Aristotle, slavery is a natural phenomenon, like being a woman. Between these two forms of subordination, there exists yet another profound similarity: 'among barbarians, the female and the slave have the same rank', because barbarians 'have no class of natural rulers'. The community that characterizes barbarian societies is a community of slaves. Aristotle cites approvingly a line from Euripides (*Iphigenia in Aulis*, line 1400): ''Tis meet that Greeks should rule barbarians.'[9]

Today, hardly anyone would claim that slavery is a natural phenomenon. Moreover, questions about the role played by cultural elements in the opposition between men and women have been around for a long time. But other statements within Aristotle's vast *oeuvre* end up contradicting those which have just been mentioned.

Once again, we are confronted with an answer to the challenge posed by sophists.

Deliberately provocative, their affirmations about the relation between *nomos* (law/constitution) and *physis* (nature) claimed human access to reality as self-evident, similar to Pindar's words, 'Custom is the queen of all things.' But Aristotle, in his *Peri hermeneias* [*On Interpretation*], focused on language and the problematic relationship between language and meaning. Referring to a statement from Plato's *The Sophist*, Aristotle observed that a noun taken alone and out of context can neither be true or false, 'unless one adds that it is or is not, absolutely speaking (*haplos*) or referring to time (*kata chronon*)'.[10] With this distinction, the issue addressed by the sophists—the distinction between *physis* (nature) and *nomos*

9 Aristotle, *Politics* [c. 325 BCE] (H. Rackham trans.) (Cambridge: Harvard University Press, 1959), 1252 a26–1252 b11.

10 Carlo Ginzburg, *Wooden Eyes: Nine Reflections on Distance* (New York: Columbia University Press, 2001) pp. 25–61.

(law/custom)—was tacitly shifted from the ontological to the epistemological level, from reality to discourse.[11]

On the surface, this argument looks purely technical; in fact, it amounted to a turning point in the history of thought, even if it was neither presented nor perceived as such for a long time. Looking back, it looks like a bomb that would end up exploding nearly two thousand years later. In his Latin translation of Aristotle's *Peri hermeneias*, Boethius (who lived between the fifth and sixth centuries CE) translated the distinction between *haplos* and *katà chronon* as *simpliciter* (absolutely) and *secundum quid* (according to the circumstances).[12] The latter term expanded to a larger scale the general characterization indicated by Aristotle.

Generation after generation of students read Aristotle's *On Interpretation* in Boethius' Latin translation (*De interpretatione*). Two of them would end up being the protagonists in the famous debate which took place in Valladolid, at the behest of Charles V, in 1550–51: Juan Ginés de Sepúlveda, translator of and commentator on Aristotle; and the Dominican friar Bartolomé de Las Casas, Bishop of Chiapas.

5. Sepúlveda and Las Casas were at odds on two issues: could one consider the Indios of the New World slaves by nature, and was a

---

11 Aristotle's distinction may have been inspired by a passage of *Dissoi logoi* 5.15, a sophist treatise; see Thomas M. Robinson, *Contrasting Arguments: An Edition of the* Dissoi Logoi (New York: Arno Press, 1979), p. 131, pp. 208–9.

12 Aristotle, *De interpretatione* (Boethius trans.) (Berlin: De Gruyter, 2014).

war against them a just war? These two questions presupposed a third: should one regard Indians as barbarians? On these questions (as well as on many others, more or less related to these), the two interlocutors took diametrically opposed positions: Sepúlveda argued for the Indios' natural inferiority, whereas Las Casas fought for their rights, making a decisive contribution (as it is widely considered today) to the idea of human rights.[13] Still, Sepúlveda and Las Casas spoke a common tongue, made up of shared cultural references: not only Aristotle, but Aristotle read through St Thomas Aquinas.

6. Thomas' reading of Aristotle was an act of intellectual appropriation that had profound intellectual and political consequences. His commentary on the first chapter of the first book of Aristotle's *Politics*, dealing with 'barbarians', was especially important. Thomas asked for a definition of 'barbarian', and then replied, quoting St Paul: 'However many the languages used in the world, all of them use sound; but if I do not understand the meaning of the sound, I am a barbarian to the person who is speaking, and the speaker is a barbarian to me.'[14]

One would be tempted to conclude, by removing this passage of Paul (who spoke Hebrew, Latin and Greek) from its context, that anyone may be a barbarian to others, regardless of who he is, as long

13 Luca Baccelli, 'Guerra e diritti: Vitoria, Las Casas e la conquista dell'America', *Quaderni fiorentini per la storia del pensiero giuridico moderno* 37 (2008): 67–101.

14 *The New Jerusalem Bible* (Henry Wansbrough ed.) (New York: Doubleday, 1985); 1 Cor 14:10–11

as he does not understand the other's language. It is difficult to imagine a more radical contestation of the idea of barbarism (and of natural barbarism) put forward by Aristotle. But Thomas did not stop there: the very interpretation of barbarism was debated. According to some, he wrote, barbarians are those who speak their language but do not know how to read or write: which is why the Venerable Bede translated the liberal arts into a vernacular language, to help the natives break free of their barbarism. Therefore, Thomas went on, by 'barbarian' one means '*aliquid extraneum*', something foreign to us: the other. It seems as if Thomas is referring back to St Paul, but instead it is Aristotle who is resurfacing: *extraneus* (other) can be meant as either *simpliciter*, absolutely, or *quo ad aliquem*, in relation to someone. From an absolute point of view, Thomas argued, we say that those who are strangers to the human race are such because they lack reason, 'or because they live in a part of the world that is not temperate' (*propter regionem aliquam intemperatam*), whose characteristics most often deprive inhabitants of intelligence, or because certain deficient customs one finds in certain lands render their inhabitants 'irrational and nearly bestial' (*irrationales et quasi brutales*). Men deprived of reason ignore both law and writing.[15]

15 Thomas Aquinas, *Commentaria* [. . .] in *octo Politicorum Aristotelis libros cum textus eiusdem: Interprete Leonardo Aretino*, colophon: '*impressum est hoc opus Romae per magistrum Eucharium Silber alias Franck, xiiii kal. Aug. 1492*', c. 4v. (I consulted the copy held at the Biblioteca Comunale degli Intronati in Siena, a–z8 A–I8).

The emergence of a geographical dimension—as imprecise as it may be—within Thomas' argumentation explains how Sepúlveda, in his *Apologia*, published in Rome in 1550, was able to cite the aforementioned page by Thomas in order to support his thesis: that war against the Indios was just.[16] Was it an unfounded reference? Certainly not, although Thomas could not foresee how his own reflections would be used almost three hundred years later to justify the Spanish conquest of the New World.

7. In the *Apologia*, Sepúlveda took up the thesis of another Latin dialogue of his, the *Democrates secundus*, that had given rise to a series of such biting critiques that it was not granted a printing.[17] In turn, Bartolomé de Las Casas responded to Sepúlveda's *Apologia*—a Spanish version of which he could have read—with a Latin *Apologia* which also went unpublished.[18] It opens with a presentation of theses by Sepúlveda, followed by an impassioned and extremely detailed refutation, starting from those concerning barbarism.

Las Casas distinguished different uses of the term 'barbarism'. According to the first, barbarism is synonymous with ferocity, and can therefore be applied to everyone, including (Las Casas observed

---

16 Juan Ginés de Sepúlveda, *Apologia Joannis Genesii Sepulvedae pro libro de iustis belli causis* in Juan Ginés de Sepúlveda and Bartolomé de Las Casas, *Apologia* (Angel Losada ed. and trans.) (Madrid: Editora Nacional, 1975[1550]).

17 Juan Ginés de Sepúlveda, *Democrate secondo ovvero sulle giuste cause di guerra* (Domenico Taranto ed.) (Macerata: Quodlibet, 2009[1544]).

18 Bartolomé de Las Casas, *Apologia* in Sepúlveda and Las Casas, *Apologia*.

contentiously) the Spanish, for the way in which they acted towards the Indios. According to the second meaning (continues Las Casas, following the commentary of St Thomas on Aristotle's *Politics*), barbarism refers to those who do not possess a written language. He who does not understand another's language is a barbarian, as St Paul says: it is in this sense that John Chrysostom may label the Three Wise Men as 'barbarians'. And Las Casas commented:[19]

> These barbarians are not barbarians *simpliciter*, absolutely, but rather barbarians *secundum quid*: and therefore they are not to be spoken of as proper barbarians, but as barbarians due to a series of accidental circumstances, *ex accidenti*.[20]

Las Casas took up the distinction introduced by Aristotle in his *Peri hermeneias*, translated by Boethius and commented upon by Thomas. Recalling this Aristotelian origin is not irrelevant. To speak of a 'traditional Thomist distinction', as Pagden did,[21] would distort the meaning of the discussion between Sepúlveda and Las Casas.

Las Casas used the distinction between *simpliciter* and *secundum quid* to distance himself from the Aristotelian Sepúlveda and his identification of the Indios with Aristotle's barbarians as 'slaves by nature'. 'It is absolutely evident,' Las Casas observed, that the 'barbarians by nature' mentioned in the first book of *Politics* have

19 Las Casas, *Apologia*, c. 15r.

20 '*Huiusmodi barbari non simpliciter sed secundum quid barbari dicuntur: hoc est non sunt proprie barbari, sed ex accidenti* [. . .]'. See Aristotle, *Politics* 1285a.

21 Pagden, *Fall of Natural Man*, p. 126.

nothing to do with the barbarian monarchies (*barbarorum regna*) talked about in the third book: kingdoms resembling tyrannies and yet different, observes Aristotle, because they 'govern according to law and are hereditary'.[22] But in the Latin *Apologia* of Las Casas, the passage from Aristotle is cited in a slightly different form: 'legitimate and conforming to the mores of the country' (*legitima et secundum morem patriae*).[23] The motive is simple: Las Casas had read a Latin version of *Politics* translated by the humanist Leonardo Bruni, offered in 1438 to Pope Eugen IV, and printed with Thomas' commentary first in Rome in 1492, then in Venice in 1500.[24] Bruni (followed by Las Casas) misunderstood the meaning of the adjective *patrikai* in Aristotle's passage,[25] linking it to the 'fatherland' (*secundum morem patriae*) rather than to the 'hereditary' transmission of the father to the son. Thomas, who had read and commented Aristotle's *Politics* in the literal translation of William of Moerbeke, did not commit such a mistake. One can assume that Bruni's mistranslation comes from another passage of Aristotle that Las

22 Aristotle, *Politics* p. 249.

23 '*apud quosdam barbaros regna vim habentia proxima tyrannidi licet sint legitima et secundum morem patriae*' (Las Casas, *Apologia*, c. 15v). Pagden translates this as: 'legitimate and paternal [in origin]' (Pagden, *Fall of Natural Man*, p. 132), going back to a passage of commentary by St Thomas that Las Casas cited in his *Apologia* (but we find no trace of this citation).

24 Cesare Vasoli, 'Leonardo Bruni' in *Dizionario biografico degli italiani*, VOL. 14 (Rome: Istituto della Enciclopedia Italiana, 1972), pp. 618–33; here, p. 629. Aquinas, *Commentaria*, c. 4v.

25 Aristotle, *Politics* 1285 a19.

Casas does not cite, in which these barbarian monarchies were identified as Asian monarchies: 'for because the barbarians are more servile in their nature (*physei*) than the Greeks, and the Asiatics than the Europeans, they endure despotic rule without any resentment'.[26]

Las Casas argued—against Aristotle, who took the natural barbarism of Asian peoples as a given—that these 'legitimate' monarchies (*katà nomon*), made possible by the 'character naturally more servile' (*physei*) of Asian populations, were merely cases of barbarism *secundum quid*.[27] In other words, Las Casas took advantage of a conceptual tool forged by Aristotle in order to distance himself from its creator, Aristotle, and his interpreter, Sepúlveda.[28]

8. Starting from the passage about the barbarian monarchies we find in the third book of Aristotle's *Politics*, Las Casas proposed a double analogy with the Indios of the New World. On the one hand, a negative analogy: the Indios are spared the stigma of absolute barbarism—barbarism *simpliciter*—to which Sepúlveda had condemned them. On the other hand, a positive analogy: like the barbarian monarchies described by Aristotle, the Indios have a 'legitimate, just and natural

26 Aristotle, *Politics*, 249.

27 Pagden (*Fall of Natural Man*, p. 236n44) writes that William of Moerbeke, followed by Las Casas, would have been guilty of a 'deliberate distortion of Aristotle's text'; but Las Casas had read a different translation.

28 Thomas Aquinas, *Commentaria*, c. 85v: '*secundum legem et secundum leges patrias. Dicunt autem leges patriae consuetudines, quae descendunt a parentibus in filios*'. See Thomas Aquinas, *In libros Politicorum Aristotelis expositio* [c. 1272 CE] (Raimondo Spiazzi ed.) (Turin: Marietti, 1951).

principle'.[29] The qualities that Las Casas famously recognized in these populations, namely, their gentleness and their ease with the mechanical arts, were in a certain sense the corollary of their identification with a relative, '*secundum quid*' barbarism.

This looks like a decisive point, because it clarifies an apparent contradiction in Las Casas' discourse. When we deal with the barbarians, he wrote, we must refrain from acts of repression, as the philosopher (that is, Aristotle) argues: we must coax them and lead them lovingly towards proper mores. Barbarians were also created in the image of God. Faced with human beings, whoever they may be—including those plunged in the most extreme barbarism—we must demonstrate Christian charity. Once again, Las Casas quoted St Paul from memory, mixing up passages from the Epistle to the Romans,[30] the Epistle to the Galatians[31] and the Epistle to the Colossians:[32]

> I have an obligation to Greeks as well as barbarians, to the educated as well as the ignorant and hence the eagerness on my part to preach the gospel [. . .] There can be [. . .] neither male nor female [. . .] there is no room for distinction between Greek and Jew, between the circumcised and uncircumcised, or between barbarian and Scythian, slave

29 Las Casas, *Apologia*, c. 22r.

30 Rom. 1:14–15

31 Gal. 3:28–29

32 Col. 3:11

> and free. There is only Christ: he is everything and he is in everything.[33]

Here, Las Casas marked an unfathomable distance between Aristotle and himself: 'Even if the philosopher, who knew neither of Christian charity nor the truth, wrote that knowledgeable people could hunt barbarians as one hunts wild beasts, nobody should think that it would be allowed to kill barbarians or treat them with harshness as if they were mares.'[34]

Las Casas is alluding to a passage from the first book of Aristotle's *Politics*. Sepúlveda had also cited it in his *Democrates secundus*, which Las Casas had been unable to read.[35] A terrible passage, which must be cited in its entirety:

> If therefore nature makes nothing without purpose or in vain, it follows that nature has made all the animals for the sake of men. Hence even the art of war will by nature be in a manner an art of acquisition (for the art of hunting is a part of it) that is properly employed both against wild animals and against such of mankind as though designed by nature for subjection refuse to submit to it, inasmuch as this warfare is by nature just.[36]

---

33 *New Jerusalem Bible.*

34 Las Casas, *Apologia*, c. 21r.

35 Sepúlveda, *Democrate*, p. 35.

36 Aristotle, *Politics* 1256 b21–27.

'Farewell, Aristotle' (*Valeat Aristoteles*) wrote Las Casas.[37] In the edition of *Politics* translated by Bruni—which Las Casas had read—the passage which I just cited was accompanied by a commentary by St Thomas. A few, laconic sentences: 'Hunting is necessary amongst beasts that are naturally subject to man, as well as against barbarian men who are naturally slaves, as one has already stated; and if such a war ever takes place, it is a just war.'[38]

St Thomas commented on Aristotle; he did not judge him. Las Casas, a just and brave man, may have read these statements with horror. But he could have never written: 'Farewell, St Thomas.'

9. Between Greek ethnocentrism and Christian universalism lies an abyss; but one must be wary of oversimplifications. Las Casas quoted the words of St Paul—before Christ, there are neither slaves

---

37 Las Casas, *Apologia*, c. 21r.

38 Aquinas, *Commentaria*, c.14r: '*et pars eius est praedativa, qua oportet uti ad bestias que naturaliter sunt subiecte hominibus et ad homines barbaros qui sunt naturaliter servi, ut supradictum est; et si hoc bellum sit* [,] *iustum secundum naturam* [*est*]'. This integration may refute the hypothesis advanced by Richard Tuck (*The Rights of War and Peace: Political Thought and the International Order from Grotius to Kant* [Oxford: Oxford University Press, 1999], pp. 71–2) according to which this version, which he quotes from the Venice edition of 1506, *c.* 9 (but the error '*secundam Naturam*' must be corrected), would be the result of an editorial intervention from the humanist era, modifying the original version: '*Ac si hoc bellum primum sit iustum secundum naturam*' (as in, for example, *Egregii doctoris sancti Thome de Aquino In libros polithicorum Ar*[*istotelis*] *comentum foeliciter incipit* [Barcelona, 1478]). Tuck refers, in a general manner, to Conor Martin, 'The Vulgate Text of Aquinas's Commentary on Aristotle's *Politics*', *Dominican Studies* 5 (1952): 35–64, an essay which remains fundamental.

nor free men—and contrasted Christian charity with the harshness of Aristotle. But Thomas, a Christian and a canonized saint as well, had not distanced himself from Aristotle, according to whom a war against slaves by nature, compared to wild beasts, is a just war. But hadn't Las Casas learnt from Aristotle himself that one could consider the Indios barbarians *secundum quid*, ruled by a power similar to tyranny yet legitimate? These are historical, not logical, contradictions.

10. Two traditions (at least) superimposed in time and space. Aristotle's *Peri hermeneias*, translated by Boethius, is an example of the way in which Greek and Latin traditions intertwined. But it is an extremely valuable example, since the distinction between *simpliciter* and *secundum quid* possesses a meta-linguistic value: it allows reflection on this intricate relationship from a distance. We may wonder whether other cultures have come up with a distinction analogous to this one. (To put it into practise in one's daily life does not necessarily imply articulating it in explicit terms.)

As I argued elsewhere, Erich Auerbach, in his essay 'Figura' (1938) reread the interpretation of the Scripture proposed by St Augustine through Erwin Panofsky's essay 'Perspective as Symbolic Form' (1924).[39] Reading the Old Testament as a part of the New Testament, as St Augustine proposed, meant emphasizing that

39 Carlo Ginzburg, 'Le forbici di Warburg' in Maria Luisa Catoni, Carlo Ginzburg, Luca Giuliani and Salvatore Settis, *Tre figure: Achille, Meleagro, Cristo* (Milan: Feltrinelli, 2013), pp. 109–32.

the Hebrew Bible had been true in the past but that its truth had been overtaken by Christian revelation. Therefore, in commenting on Augustine's reading (which ended up, via Hegel, contributing to form our own attitude with regard to history), I proposed the metaphor of 'perspective'—even if the metaphors used by Augustine are musical, not visual.[40] This perspectivism implies a hierarchy, as in Christianity's self-definition as *Verus Israel*. Could we broaden this conclusion to perspective understood at a literal level?

11. The answer to these questions leads us, once again, to the distinction articulated by Aristotle, translated by Boethius and commented by Thomas: the distinction between *simpliciter* and *secundum quid*. I cite it here in Latin, in Boethius' translation, because that is what Las Casas did in several instances. He did it also in discussing a most delicate issue: human sacrifices practised by the Indios. Indeed, in commenting on this passage, Tzvetan Todorov spoke,[41] with a certain embarrassment, of 'perspectivism': 'it is truly surprising to see "perspectivism" introduced into a field so inappropriate for it.'

But let us look more closely at what Las Casas wrote. I will cite a brief excerpt from his response to objections addressed to him by Sepúlveda during the Valladolid debate:

---

40 Ginzburg, *Wooden Eyes*, p. 155.

41 Tzvetan Todorov, *La Conquête de l'Amérique* (Paris: Seuil, 1982), p. 195.

> As for what he [Sepúlveda] says about the probable opinion, etc., I say that when any population, whatever it may be, argues about the probable opinion, it does not do so with regard to the rules of *simpliciter* reason, but because it seems to the population that it is the way to go, and that the argument is used and approved by those who are experts in an activity or art, even if they end up being mistaken.[42]

In other words, Las Casas considers human sacrifices from a *secundum quid* perspective, which, however, presupposes an absolute perspective (*simpliciter*), founded on the rules of reason—and not on those of Christian religion.

12. This link between *simpliciter* and *secundum quid* is implicit in a text which was able to unfold in the most profound way the implications of the linear perspective as cognitive model, i.e. the dedicatory epistle which precedes Niccolò Machiavelli's *The Prince*:

> Nor do I want it to be reputed presumption if a man from a low and mean state dares to discuss and give rules for the government of princes. For just as those who sketch landscapes place themselves down in the plain to consider the nature of mountains and high places and to consider the nature of low places place themselves high atop mountains, similarly, to know well the nature of peoples one needs to be

---

42 Bartolomé de Las Casas, *Obras completes, Volume 10: Tratados de 1552* (Ramón Hernández and Lorenzo Galmés eds) (Madrid: Alianza, 1992[1552]), p. 178.

prince, and to know well the nature of princes one needs to be of the people.[43]

Once upon a time, the words 'sketch landscapes' were interpreted as an allusion to Leonardo da Vinci, whom Machiavelli had met in Imola, at the court of Cesare Borgia, in 1503. But Machiavelli also definitely had in mind Aristotle's *Politics*, read (as Las Casas had done) in Bruni's Latin translation, commented by St Thomas. Perspective, far from being egalitarian, is truly hierarchical, and allows us to grasp the 'effectual truth of the thing' (*verità effettuale della cosa*) from a specific point of view. Machiavelli, one could say, integrated *simpliciter* and *secundum quid*.[44]

13. But what about the barbarism of today? Massive migratory currents have been mixing human beings from different cultures. How should we face this diversity? One can imagine two opposing attitudes: to impose our point of view, or to tolerate all behaviours whatever they may be, even those the most removed from our own. Neither of these two solutions seems satisfactory; but a poorly sketched compromise between the two seems even less so. The only acceptable solution seems to be a *secundum quid* behaviour, on a case-by-case basis. Here, casuistry may prove to be helpful. Struck dead by Pascal's *Provinciales*, casuistry (the Jesuits', but others' as

---

43 Niccolò Machiavelli, *The Prince* (Harvey C. Mansfield trans.) (Chicago: University of Chicago Press, 1998[1513]), p. 4.

44 Carlo Ginzburg, 'Intricate Readings: Machiavelli, Aristotle, Thomas Aquinas', *Journal of the Warburg and Courtauld Institutes* 78 (2015): 157–72.

well), came back to life in the context of bioethics.[45] Bioethics teaches us that the Islamic veil and genital mutilation (to take two examples) cannot be placed on the same level. We must learn from the Jesuits, and from Pascal.

45 I reflected on these subjects in the Tanner Lectures I gave at Harvard in 2015: 'Casuistry, For and Against: Pascal's *Provinciales* and Their Aftermath'.

Acknowledgements | I would like to thank Maria Luisa Catoni and Sergio Landucci for their critical remarks, and Allen Boxer for his translation. A preliminary French version of this text was presented at the MuCEM de Marseille on 13 March 2014, as part of the cycle 'Civilization and Barbarism', organized by Tzvetan Todorov.

FIGURE 1 (LEFT): Parmigianino, *Self-Portrait with a Bitch.*

FIGURE 2 (RIGHT): School of Giulio Bonasone, *Portrait of Parmigianino.*

The Soul of Brutes

A SIXTEENTH-CENTURY DEBATE[1]

1. I will begin with Parmigianino's *Self-Portrait with a Bitch*, reproduced here as Figure 1 on the facing page. This splendid drawing, now at the British Museum, is probably a self-portrait.[2] The painter, Francesco Mazzola, nicknamed Parmigianino (he was born in Parma in 1503 and died in Casalmaggiore, a nearby town, in 1540), has depicted himself holding a bitch. The identification is supported (as A. E. Popham convincingly suggested) by the physical resemblance between the sitter and a portrait representing Parmigianino in his later years.

By the time of the later portrait, the *Portrait of Parmigianino* by the School of Giulio Bonasone (see Figure 2), according to Vasari's

1 First presented at Berkeley, 21 April 2004. Many thanks are due to Franco Bacchelli for his generous help.

2 A. E. Popham, *Catalogue of the Drawings of Parmigianino*, VOL. 1 (New Haven, CT, and London: Yale University Press, 1973), pp. 108–09.

vivid description, the gentle-looking painter had developed an obsession with alchemy and become 'a sort of wild man, with a long beard and dishevelled hair'.[3]

Parmigianino was an extraordinary draughtsman, skilled in all media—from wash to pencil, from red chalk to pen. In the *Self-Portrait*, the fluid, sensitive line conveys the physical and emotional closeness between two very different beings: the sitting man and the standing, pregnant bitch.

A much-quoted passage from Ovid's *Metamorphoses*, echoed by Augustine and innumerable Christian writers after him, explained that God gave man an upturned face, 'os sublime dedit', as a sign of his pre-eminence in the cosmos.[4] I would argue that, in portraying himself (or perhaps somebody else) besides a standing bitch, Parmigianino meant to ironically undermine the ancient commonplace which took the erect stance of human beings as a proof of their excellence.

But is such an interpretation convincing? Are we entitled to read a philosophical message in a drawing that appears to depict nothing but a cosy domestic scene? I think we are. My argument relies upon

---

3 *Parma per l'arte*, Issue 3 (1953), facing p. 10. See Giorgio Vasari, *Le opere di Giorgio Vasari*, VOL. 5 (Gaetano Milanesi ed.) (Firenze: Sansoni, 1976[1906]), p. 233: 'ed essendo di delicato e gentile, fatto con la barba e chiome lunghe e malconce'.

4 Carlo Ginzburg, 'The High and the Low' in *Clues, Myths, and the Historical Method* (John Tedeschi and Anne Tedeschi trans) (Baltimore, MD: Johns Hopkins University Press, 2013), pp. 54–69.

an etching in chiaroscuro by Ugo da Carpi (see Figure 3), based on a (now lost) drawing that Parmigianino, as we learn from Vasari, either made in Bologna or brought to Bologna in 1527, after Rome—where he had spent a few years—had been sacked.[5]

In Figure 4, the same subject is explicitly declared in a much cruder version by Giulio Bonasone as one of the many emblems illustrating Achille Bocchi's *Symbolicarum quaestionum de universo genere quas serio ludebat libri quinque* (Five Books of Symbolical Questions on All Sort of Subjects, of Which He Made a Serious Game), first published in Bologna in 1555. Bocchi's related poem praises endurance in front of the hardships of human life.

The caption in Figure 4—'Hic est homo Platonis'—refers to an anecdote concerning Diogenes the Cynic, told by Diogenes Laertius in his *Lives of Philosophers*: 'Plato had defined man as an animal, biped and featherless, and was applauded. Diogenes plucked a fowl and brought it into the lecture-room with the words, "Here is Plato's man." '[6]

5 Vasari, *Le opera*, VOL. 5, p. 226: 'nel qual tempo fece intagliare alcune stampe di chiaroscuro, e fra l'altre la Decollazione di San Piero e San Paulo, ed un Diogene grande'.

6 Diogenes Laertius, *Lives of the Eminent Philosophers*, VOL. 2 (Robert D. Hicks trans.) (Cambridge, MA: Harvard University Press, 1979), BOOK 6, p. 40. See Edgar Wind, 'Homo Platonis', *Journal of the Warburg* 1(3) (1937–38): 261.

FIGURE 3 (LEFT): Ugo da Carpi, *Diogenes*.

FIGURE 4 (RIGHT): Achille Bocchi, *Symbolicarum Quaestionum*.

Images illustrating this anecdote are exceedingly rare.[7] Parmigianino's unusual choice may have been inspired by a learned patron familiar either with Diogenes Laertius' *Lives of the Philosophers* or with two short texts by Erasmus dealing with the same subject.[8] Although the passage I am talking about is not included in the Italian shortened versions of Laertius' *Lives*, I would not entirely rule out the possibility that the subject was chosen by Parmigianino himself.[9]

Parmigianino's letters and contracts, in which grammatical peculiarities certainly do crop up, are nonetheless written in a regular, educated hand (see Figure 5, overleaf).[10]

---

7 Andor Pigler, *Barockthemen: eine Auswahl von Verzeichnissen zur Ikonographie des 17. und 18. Jahrhunderts*, VOL. 2 (Budapest: Akademiai Kiado, 1974). See Andor Pigler, 'The Importance of Iconographical Exactitude', *The Art Bulletin* XXI (1939): 228–37; particularly p. 234.

8 Desiderius Erasmus, *Apophthegmata* in *Opera* (Jean Le Clerc ed.) (Lugduni Batavorum Vander, 1706), VOL. 4, p. 178; see also Desiderius Erasmus, 'Socratis gallus aut callus' in *Adagia* in *Opera*, VOL. 2, p. 1192.

9 Diogenes Laertius, *Vite de philosophi moralissime et de le loro elegantissime sententie extratte da Laertio et altri antiquissimi authori historiate et di novo corrette in lingua tosca* (Nicolo Zoppino ed. and trans.) (Venice: Nicolò Zopino and Vincentio campagno, 1524), CHAPTER 49 on Diogenes the Cynic. See also Diogenes Laertius, *El libro della vita de philosophi et delle loro elegantissime sententie extracto da D. Lahertio et da altri antiquissimi auctori* (Florence: Franciscum de Bonaccursiis et Antonium Venetum, 1488).

10 Lucia Fornari Schianchi and Sylvia Ferino Pagden (eds), *Parmigianino e il manierismo europeo* (Milan: Silvana, 2004), p. 172. Later accounts about Parmigianino's accomplished humanistic education (p. 414) hardly seem believable.

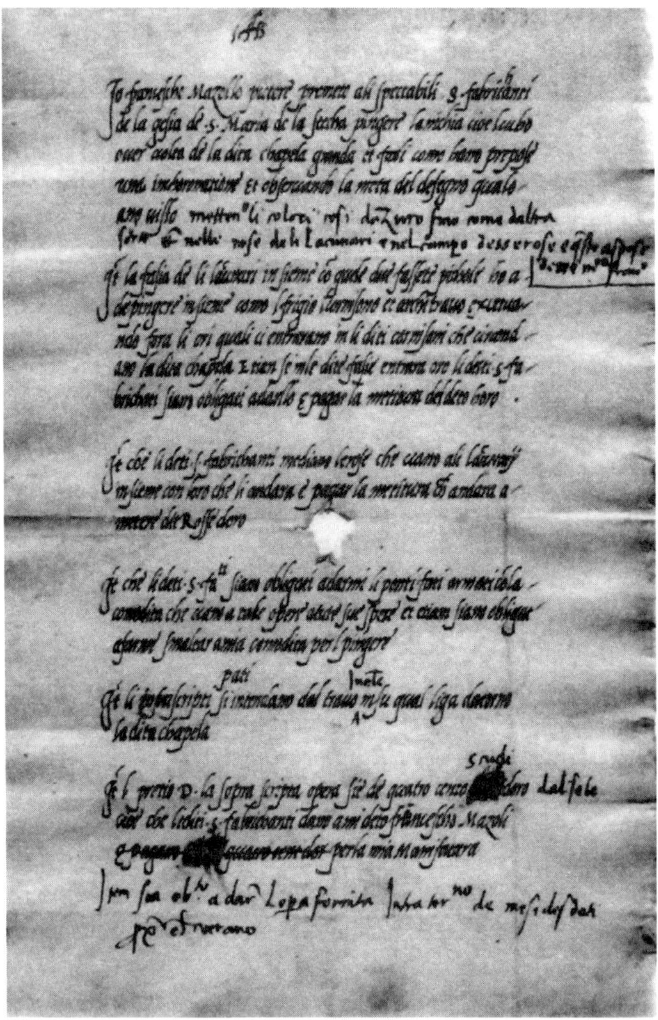

FIGURE 5: Parmigianino's contract, 1531 (Santa Maria della Steccata, Parma).

Diogenes' aggressive caricature of Plato's man resembles the point Parmigianino made, in a more intimate mode, by portraying himself close to the standing bitch.[11] In both cases, the uniqueness of human beings was cast into doubt by stressing their similarity with allegedly inferior animals.

2. Parmigianino's striking images are a fitting introduction to my topic: the sixteenth-century debate on the souls of brutes. My emphasis on the sixteenth rather than the seventeenth century, needs some clarification. In two articles of his *Dictionnaire historique et critique* (1696–97), Pierre Bayle compellingly showed that the later debate was a response to Descartes's theory of *animaux-machines*, beasts as automata. Significantly, however, Bayle's most profound reflections on the subject can be found in the article that appears under the heading 'Rorarius': the Latinized name of a sixteenth-century writer, Girolamo Rorario, whose posthumously published dialogue helped trigger the debate.[12]

The crucial role played by the adjective '*bruta*' in the title of Rorario's dialogue—*Quod animalia bruta sepe ratione utantur melius*

---

11 Patrizia Pinotti, 'Gli animali in Platone' in Silvana Castignone and Giuliana Lanata (eds), *Filosofia e animali nel mondo antico* (Pisa: ETS, 1994), p. 120.

12 Pierre Bayle, *Dictionnaire historique et critique* (Basel: Chez Jean Louis Brandmuller, 1741), VOL. 3, 'Pereira', pp. 649–56; VOL. 1, 'Rorarius', pp. 76–87. Rorario's importance was stressed by Eugenio Garin, *Storia della filosofia italiana*, VOL. 2 (Turin: Einaudi, 1966), pp. 912–14; see also Eugenio Garin, *Dal Rinascimento all'Illuminismo* (Pisa: Nistri-Lischi, 1970), pp. 176–8.

homine (Brutes Are Often More Rational than Men)—is perhaps not self-evident to a twenty-first century reader. Equally puzzling might be the words with which Francesca da Rimini addresses the poet in the fifth canto of Dante's *Inferno*: '*o animal grazïoso e benigno*' (Lo! gracious and benevolent animal).[13] We tend to forget that, for a long time, animals meant 'all beings endowed with sensation and voluntary motion'. This definition, still echoed in the *Shorter Oxford English Dictionary*, usually did not imply any equality: one has simply to recall Hamlet's words, 'What a piece of work is Man. [. . .] The Parragon of animals.'[14] Today, those who speak of 'animal rights' employ a different language.

This linguistic disjunction conceals a contiguity in content. The debate on the souls of brutes dealt with issues which still (or, possibly, once again) resonate with us. A recapitulation of the roots of this debate in the Greek philosophical tradition is necessary, in order to see how they shaped the sixteenth-century perception—and, indirectly, ours.

3. In a famous passage of his *Nicomachean Ethics*, Aristotle asked: What is the specific function (*ergon*) of man? Not life, he answered, which man shares with all living beings, including plants; not sensation, which man shares with the horse, the ox and other

13 Dante Alighieri, *La Commedia, Volume II*: *Inferno* (Giorgio Petrocchi ed.) (Milan: Mondadori, 1966–67), 5.88.

14 William Shakespeare, *Hamlet* (Ann Thompson and Neil Taylor eds) (London: Arden Shakespeare, 2020), 2.2.20.

animals; man's specific function is reason (*logos*), both practical and theoretical.[15] Therefore, since 'rational, or at least not irrational activity seems to be the function of man', Aristotle identified man as a rational animal: a definition which mirrored, on a technical level, the Greek word for 'the other animals' that is, brutes: *ta aloga*, 'those without reason'.[16]

In his *Politics*, Aristotle spelt out the implications of man's supremacy:

> Clearly we must suppose [. . .] that plants exist for the sake of animals and the other animals for the good of man, the domestic species both for his service and for his food, and if not all, at all events most of the wild ones for the sake of his food and of his supplies of other kinds, in order that they may furnish him both with clothing and with other appliances. If therefore nature makes nothing without purpose or in vain, it follows that nature has made all the animals for the sake of men.[17]

Hunting, as a form of war, Aristotle concluded, 'is by nature just'.

15 Aristotle, *Nicomachean Ethics* 1097b24–1098a18.
16 Émile Benveniste, *Il vacabolario delle istituzioni indoeuropee*, VOL. 1 (M. Liborio ed. and trans.) (Turin: Einaudi, 1976), p. 26.
17 Aristotle, *Politics* (H. Rackham trans.) (Cambridge: Harvard University Press, 1959), 1256 b15–27.

The entirety of the natural world ultimately exists for the sake of man. But man's position in the natural world is not based on the possession of a soul. At the beginning of his treatise *On the Soul*, Aristotle complained that 'speakers and inquirers about the soul seem today to confine their inquiries to the soul of man. But,' he objected:

> one must be careful not to evade the question whether one definition of 'soul' is enough, as we can give one definition of 'living creature', or whether there must be a different one in each case; that is, one of the horse, one of the dog, one of man, and one of God, and whether the words 'living creature' as a common term have no meaning, or logically come later.[18]

Then Aristotle distinguished among different faculties of the soul:

> some living things [. . .] have all, others only some, and others again only one. Those which we have mentioned are the faculties for nourishment, for appetite, for sensation, for movement in space, and for thought.[19]

We have a sort of ladder, with man—the only animal capable of thought—at the top. But Aristotle perceived a notable difficulty, which he promised to deal with later: 'the question of imagination'

18 Aristotle, *On the Soul. Parva Naturalia. On Breath* (W. S. Hett trans.) (Cambridge, MA: Harvard University Press, 1957, Loeb Classical Library 288), 402b7.
19 Aristotle, *On the Soul* 414a29–414a33.

(*phantasia*) which he declared 'obscure'.[20] But the long discussion he devoted to *phantasia* in the third book of the treatise *On the Soul* did not clarify the issue.[21] His notion of *phantasia* remains obscure and occasionally contradictory—which is possibly the only point of agreement between many recent, largely divergent interpretations.[22]

An adequate comment on this intricate issue is beyond my competence. I will limit myself to underlining a few points closely related to my topic.

---

20 Aristotle, *On the Soul* 414b17–188.

21 Aristotle, *On the Soul* 427b29–429a9.

22 Martha C. Nussbaum, 'The Role of *Phantasia* in Aristotle's Explanations of Action' in *Aristotle's De Motu Animalium* (Martha C. Nussbaum ed.) (Princeton, NJ: Princeton University Press, 1978), pp. 221–69; Malcolm Schofield, 'Aristotle on the Imagination' in Martha C. Nussbaum and Amelie Oksenberg Rorty (eds), *Essays on Aristotle's* De Anima (Oxford: Clarendon Press, 1992), pp. 249–77; Dorothea Frede, 'The Cognitive Role of *Phantasia* in Aristotle' in *Essays on Aristotle's De Anima*, pp. 279–95. A good survey is provided by Giorgio Camassa, '*Phantasia* da Platone ai Neoplatonici' in Marta Fattori and Massimo Bianchi (eds), *Phantasia-Imaginatio* (Rome: Edizioni dell'Ateneo, 1988), pp. 24–55. See also Gerald Watson, 'Φαντασία in Aristotle, *De Anima* 3.3', *The Classical Quarterly* 32(1) (1982): 100–13; Deborah Modrak, 'Φαντασία Reconsidered', *Archiv für die Geschichte der Philosophie* 68(1) (1986): 47–69; Jean-Louise Labarrière, 'Imagination humaine et imagination animale chez Aristote', *Phronesis* 29(1) (1984): 17–49; Jean-Louise Labarrière, 'Raison humaine et intelligence animale dans la philosophie grecque', *Terrain* 34 (March 2000) (*Les animaux pensent-ils?*): 107–22. On the general issue, see Richard Sorabji, *Animal Minds and Human Morals: The Origins of the Western Debate* (Ithaca, NY: Cornell University Press, 1993).

(1) For Aristotle, *phantasia* seems to be something in between sensation (*aisthesis*) and thought (*noesis*), as well as sensation and desire: a meaning approximately conveyed by the words 'reproductive imagination' (*phantasia* began to indicate 'productive imagination' only much later).[23]

(2) Aristotle denies that *phantasia* is shared by 'all animals': 'this appears not to be the case; for instance, it is true of the ant and the bee, not of the worm.'[24] This passage, 428a11, is corrupt and, according to the manuscript tradition, should be read as 'for instance, it is not true of the ant, of the bee, of the worm'—which does not make much sense. Note that Aquinas' commentary on this passage, based on William of Moerbeke's translation of the traditional text, somewhat anticipated Torstrik's textual correction which I followed.[25]

(3) The aforementioned passage seems to imply that some brutes, having *phantasia*, are closer to man; but Aristotle[26] introduces a

---

23 Camassa, '*Phantasia* da Platone ai Neoplatonici', p. 50 (quoting Philostratus, *Life of Apollonius* 6.19).

24 Aristotle, *On the Soul* 428a11.

25 Aristotle, *L'anima* (Giancarlo Movia ed.) (Naples: Luigi Loffredo, 1979), 428a10–12; Labarrière, 'Imagination': 23. Interestingly, in his commentary on *De anima* Aquinas opposed ants' and bees' *phantasia indeterminata* to worms' lack of *phantasia*, although the text translated by William of Moerbeke listed the three species together: see Thomas Aquinas, *Sancti Thomae Aquinatis In Aristotelis librum de Anima commentarium* (Angelo M. Pirotta ed.) (Casale: Marietti, 1979), p. 159.

26 Aristotle, *On the Soul* 3.10.

further distinction between sensitive imagination (*aisthetike phantasia*) on the one hand, and calculating and deliberative imagination (*logistike phantasia, bouleutike phantasia*) on the other: the former is shared by all living creatures, the latter only by man.[27] 'Hence,' Aristotle concludes, 'appetite (*orexis*) does not imply capacity for deliberation (*to bouleutikon*)': the choice of a greater good can be made only through the use of the syllogism, hence only by rational animals.

4. By introducing the notion of *phantasia*, Aristotle somewhat blurred the clear-cut distinction he suggested elsewhere between rational and non-rational animals. The long-term impact of his thoughts on this subject are particularly evident in the writings of Plutarch, the most influential advocate of the rationality of animals in the Greek philosophical tradition. Plutarch repeatedly quoted from Aristotle's zoological writings (especially *History of Animals*): moreover, and more importantly, he developed, and occasionally modified, concepts put forward by Aristotle, especially in his treatise *On the Soul*. Plutarch's argumentative strategy was dictated by his target: the Stoic philosophers, and their emphasis on reason and language as elements which sharply opposed man to all other animals.

In his dialogue *Whether Land or Sea Animals are Cleverer*, usually referred as *De sollertia animalium*, Plutarch started from Aristotle's

---

27 Aristotle, *On the Soul* 433b24–30.

argument that all animals possessed imagination (*phantasia*) and sensation (*aisthesis*), then added reason to the list:

> But if it is ridiculous that within the class of living things there must be an antithesis between sentient and insentient, or an antithesis between imaginative and unimaginative, since it is the nature of every creature with a soul to be sentient and imaginative from the hour of its birth, so he, also, is unreasonable who demands a division among the living into a rational and an irrational group.[28]

Through Autobulos, his mouthpiece in the dialogue, Plutarch placed himself firmly among those who:

> believe that nothing is endowed with sensation which does not also partake of intelligence and that there is no living thing which does not naturally possess both opinion and reason [*doxa tis kai logismos*], just as it has sensation and appetite. For nature, which they rightly say, does everything with some purpose and to some end, did not create the sentient nature [*to zoon aisthetikon*] merely to be sentient when something happens to it.[29]

The words 'they rightly say' have been interpreted as an allusion to Aristotle. And Plutarch made an explicit reference to one of

---

28 Plutarch, *Moralia*, VOL. 12 (Harold F. Cherniss and William C. Helmbold trans) (Cambridge, MA: Harvard University Press, 1957), 960D–E.

29 Plutarch, *Moralia* 960C–E.

Aristotle's followers, Strato of Lampsachus: 'There is, in fact, a work of Strato, the natural philosopher, which proves that it is impossible to have sensation at all without some action of the intelligence.'[30]

5. A short digression may be appropriate at this point. Strato of Lampsacus, born about 330, died about 270 BCE. He was often referred to as a natural philosopher (*physikos*), and Plutarch called him such. Strato wrote about such things as void and acceleration, zoology and psychology; but only fragments of his extensive work survive. According to the historian Polybius, Strato excelled in dismantling other thinkers' arguments but was much less convincing when the time came to advance his own.[31] Others spoke of Strato's originality and intellectual independence, specifically vis-à-vis Aristotle, his teacher.

Strato's reflections on the soul attracted Plutarch's attention; I wonder whether a passage from Aristotle's *Politics* might have contributed to these thoughts.[32] Since, from Plato onwards, all

---

30 Plutarch, *Moralia* 961A–B. See Strato of Lampsacus, *Straton von Lampsakos* (Fritz Wehrli ed.), Die Schule des Aristoteles, Texte und Kommentar, V (Basel: Schwabe, 1950), fragment 112. See on this passage Margherita Isnardi Parente, 'Le obiezioni di Stratone al "Fedone" e l'epistemologia peripatetica nel primo ellenismo', *Rivista di filologia e istruzione classica* 105 (1977): 287–306. See also Luciana Repici, *La natura e l'anima: Saggi su Stratone di Lampsaco* (Turin: Tirrenia Stampatori, 1988); Julia Annas, *Hellenistic Philosophy of Mind* (Berkeley: University of California Press, 1992), pp. 28–30.

31 Strato, *Straton von Lampsakos*, fragment 112.

32 Repici, *La natura e l'anima*.

discourses on the soul were also, at least implicitly, discourses on the body politic, I am surprised that the debate over the souls of brutes has apparently never turned to the famous analogy, put forward by Aristotle in his *Politics*, between 'the other animals' (that is, brutes) and slaves. Let me recall a couple of passages:

> [. . .] all men that differ as widely as the soul does from the body and the human being from the lower animal (and this is the condition of those whose function is the use of the body and from whom this is the best that is forthcoming) these are by nature slaves.[33]

Aristotle compared slaves first to lower (literally, wild) animals (*theria*); then to 'the other animals' (*ta alla zoa*), finally to 'domestic animals' (*emera zoa*):

> For he is by nature a slave who is capable of belonging to another (and that is why he does so belong) and who participates in reason so far as to apprehend it but not to possess it; for the animals other than man are subservient not to reason, by apprehending it, but to feelings [*to gar alla zoa ou logo aisthanomena alla pathemasin uperetei*]. And also the usefulness of slaves diverges little from that of animals; bodily service for the necessities of life is forthcoming from both, from slaves and from domestic animals alike.[34]

33 Aristotle, *Politics* 1254b16–20.

34 Aristotle, *Politics* 1254b20–28; see also 1280a24–25; 1281b19–21.

Today Aristotle's words sound offensive; they clearly refer to a society which is different from ours. But is it possible that Aristotle's dehumanizing gaze prodded someone to think in a very different direction? I wonder whether Strato's argument, mentioned by Plutarch, that 'it is impossible to have sensation at all [*aisthanestai to parapan*] without some action of the intelligence' might have sprung from a reversal of Aristotle's analogy between slaves and brutes, both of whom he called 'subservient not to reason and its apprehension, but to feelings [*pathemasin*]'. The criticism, either implicit or explicit, would have been precisely what Aristotle himself made when he repeatedly warned about the dangers of analogy.[35] It is my opinion that Strato submitted the middle term of the analogy—sensations—to a closer scrutiny. Relying on the same verb, *aisthánomai* (to perceive), Aristotle degraded some humans, and Strato, reinterpreted by Plutarch, promoted some brutes.

6. I say 'some brutes' because Plutarch, in *Whether Land or Sea Animals are Cleverer*, repeatedly insisted that there are wide differences among humans as well as among 'the other animals'. He employed Strato's argument against some unnamed 'logicians' (*dialektikoi*). One of Plutarch's targets was Chrysippus, the Stoic philosopher, who asserted:

35 G. E. R. Lloyd, *Polarity and Analogy: Two Types of Argumentation in Early Greek Thought* (Cambridge: Cambridge University Press, 1971), pp. 361–83.

> that when a dog arrives at a point where the path branches into many, he makes use of a multiple disjunctive argument and reasons with himself: 'Either the wild beast has taken this path, or this one, or this one. But surely it has not taken this one, or this one. Then it must have gone by the remaining road.' Perception here affords nothing but the minor premise, while the force of reason gives the major premises and adds the conclusion to the premises.[36]

As we learn from Sextus Empiricus,[37] Chrysippus, who was 'particularly hostile to irrational animals', argued that the dog was 'implicitly reasoning'.[38] Plutarch made fun of this conclusion:

> A dog, however, does not need such testimonial, which is both false and fraudulent; for it is perception itself, relying on track and spoor, that indicates the way the creature fled; it does not bother with disjunctive and copulative propositions.[39]

Plutarch put forward a counter-example:

> Even to this day the Thracians, whenever they consider crossing a frozen river, rely on a vixen to determine how solid the ice is. The vixen moves ahead slowly and presses

36 Plutarch, *Moralia* 969A–B.

37 Sextus Empiricus, *Outlines of Scepticism* (Julia Annas and Jonathan Barnes trans and eds) (Cambridge: Cambridge University Press, 1994), 6.62–72.

38 Empiricus, *Outlines of Scepticism* 1, 69.

39 Plutarch, *Moralia* 969B

> her ear to the ice; if she perceives by the sound that the stream is running close underneath, she concludes that the frozen part is not very thick, but rather thin and dangerous, and so stands stock-still and, if she is permitted, returns to the shore; but if there is no noise, she is reassured and crosses over. And let us not declare that this is a nicety of perception unaided by reason; it is, rather, a syllogistic conclusion developed from the evidence of perception: 'What makes noise must be in motion; what is in motion is not frozen; what is not frozen is liquid; what is liquid gives way.'[40]

To defeat the disjunctive propositions of Chrysippus' dog, Plutarch proposed a syllogistic fox. [41]

7. *Whether Land or Sea Animals are Cleverer* is the longest and most important of a number of writings Plutarch devoted to the condition of beasts. They were all included in the great Greek edition of Plutarch's *Moralia* Aldo Manuzio published in Venice in 1509. But the most influential of these pieces, *Beasts Are Rational*, had by that date already begun to circulate in Latin, in two different translations. The first was printed in Brescia in 1503 as an independent booklet; the translator, Domenico Bonomini, was unable to decide

---

40 Plutarch, *Moralia* 969A.

41 For a different interpretation of this passage, see Labarrière, 'Raison humaine': 117–18.

whether its author was Plutarch or Lucian. The second was published in Venice in 1508 along with a selection of Plutarch's other shorter works, under the title *Dialogus in quo animalia bruta ratione uti monstrantur*.[42] In *Beasts Are Rational*, Plutarch presents Ulysses in conversation with one of his former companions, Gryllus, whom Circe has transformed into a swine. Ulysses tries to convince Gryllus to rejoin the human race, but with no success. Gryllus objects that 'the soul of beasts has a greater natural capacity and perfection for the generation of virtue';[43] beasts are closer to nature; their lives are 'free from empty illusions'. Ulysses calls Gryllus 'a sophist'; Gryllus retorts: 'since I have entered into this new body of mine, I marvel at those arguments by which the sophists used to convince me that all creatures except man were *irrational and senseless*' (*aloga kai anoeta*).[44] By 'sophists', Plutarch meant, once again, the Stoics. Gryllus concludes that if one refuses to call 'the wisdom of animals [*therion phronesin*] "wisdom", it is high time for you to cast about for some fairer and even more honourable term to describe it.'[45]

42 Plutarch, *Plutarchi Chironei Dialogus* (Dominicus Bonominus trans.) (Brescia: Angelum Britannicum, 27 May 1503) (BUB: Aula V. Tab I . F. I. VOL. 423.2, bound with Isocrates, *De regno gubernando*); Plutarch, *Regum et imperatorum Apophtegmata Raphaele Regio interprete; Plutarchi Laconica apophtegmata Raphaele Regio interprete; Plutarchi Dialogus in quo animalia bruta ratione uti monstrantur, Joanne Regio interprete; Raphaelis Regii apologia, in qua quattuor hae questiones potissimum edisseruntur . . .* (Venice: Georgio Rusconi, 11 October 1508) (Vatican: Incun. IV. 573 (3)).

43 Plutarch, *Moralia* 987B.

44 Plutarch, *Moralia* 992C (emphasis added).

45 Plutarch, *Moralia* 991F.

Plutarch's playful dialogue had a considerable impact in sixteenth-century Italy. It will suffice to recall two works: Machiavelli's unfinished poem *L'asino d'oro* (*The Golden Ass*), which—notwithstanding its title, possibly a later addition—is more indebted to Plutarch than to Apuleius, and Giovan Battista Gelli's lively dialogues *La Circe*.[46] Also indebted to Plutarch's dialogue, as its title makes clear, was a work by Gerolamo Rorario, a former papal nuncio: *Quod animalia bruta sepe ratione utuntur melius homine* (Beasts Often Use Reason Better than Humans). In Rorario's dialogue, a conversation between the author and Bernardo Clesio, Bishop of Trent, framed a series of stories showing the manifold ingenuity of animals: dogs that had learnt to wait for the completion of their owners' prayers before approaching them; parrots that knew the Christian Credo by heart; dancing bears; pious elephants (mentioned by Plutarch); and so on. Rorario richly enjoyed rehearsing anecdotes from his long diplomatic career, dropping as many names as he could—of cardinals, popes, emperors. This chatty, erratic little work, begun in 1543, was probably finished in 1546.[47] In the

46 Niccolo Machiavelli, *Opere letterarie* (Luigi Blasucci ed.) (Milan: Adelphi, 1964), pp. 263–300 (see especially the last two chapters, 7 and 8); Giambattista Gelli, *La Circe* in *Dialoghi* (Roberto Tissoni ed.) (Bari: Laterza, 1967).

47 Silvano Cavazza, 'Girolamo Rorario e il dialogo "Julius exclusus"', *Memorie storiche forogiuliesi* 60 (1980): 129–64; especially 57n56 (quoting a letter Rorario addressed to Pietro Paolo Gualtieri, dated Pordenone, August 10, 1543); Pio Paschini, 'Un pordenonese nunzio papale nel secolo XVI: Gerolamo Rorario', *Memorie storiche forogiuliesi* 30 (1934): 169–216; especially 198 (for the date 1546).

meantime, Rorario (if he did not read Greek) might have taken advantage of an Italian translation, via Latin, of Plutarch's *Whether Land or Sea Animals are Cleverer*, published in Venice in 1545: *Dialogo* [. . .] *circa l'avertire de gl'animali quali sieno più accorti, o li terrestri, o li marini.*[48]

Rorario dedicated his own dialogue first to Cristoforo Madruzzo, Bishop of Trent, and then, in 1547, to Antoine Perrenot de Granvelle, Bishop of Arras. The work was apparently ready to be printed; for reasons unknown, it remained unpublished for a century. Did somebody object to the dangerous implications of its topic, notwithstanding Rorario's light, anecdotal approach? Perhaps. In any case, when the work was first published in Paris in 1648, the disappearance from the title of the adverb *sepe* (often) maliciously emphasized the unqualified superiority of brutes over men. The editor, Gabriel Naudé, was a well-known writer, a prominent member of the circle of scholars known for their irreligiosity: the so-called *libertins érudits*. In a dedicatory letter to the antiquarian Pierre Dupuy and his brother Jacques, Naudé explained that he had come across a manuscript of Rorario's dialogue fortuitously during his stay in Italy at the court of Cardinal Bagni.[49] A second edition, mentioned in Bayle's article 'Rorarius', was published in Amsterdam

48 Plutarch, *Dialogo di Plutarco circa l'avertire de gl'animali quali sieno più accorti, o li terrestri, o li marini, di greco in latino et di latino in volgare, nuovamente tradotto, et con ogni diligentia stampato* (Venice: 1545) (BUB: A. V. Caps. 17. 8).

49 Hieronymus Rorarius, *Quod animalia bruta ratione utuntur melius homine*, 2 VOLS (Gabriel Naudé ed.) (Paris: Sébastien Cramoisy, 1648) (Archig.: 10. bb. II. I. op. 3).

in 1654 and reissued in 1666. A third edition appeared in 's-Hertogenbosch in 1702; a fourth, with an erudite commentary by Ribovius, in Helmstadt, 1728.[50] One of the participants in the ensuing debate on the soul of brutes was Leibniz.

This staggering impact was utterly out of proportion with the intrinsic weight of Rorario's dialogue. But it attracted the attention of so many erudites that Rorario's life and writings are now fairly well known. He was born in Sacile, a little town near Pordenone, in Friuli, in 1485. In his early youth, he was educated by two distinguished humanists, Francesco Amalteo and Marc'Antonio Sabellico, before studying law in Padua, where he took his degree. He spent some years serving Emperor Maximilian as a diplomat; received the title of protonotary apostolic from Pope Leo X; and in 1521, travelled to Germany as Emperor Charles V's ambassador, charged with confronting the turmoil generated by Luther's religious revolt. After some time spent in Rome, at the court of Pope Clement VII (where, incidentally, he might have met Parmigianino), Rorario acted as papal nuncio in Germany, Hungary and Poland. He died in or around 1556, without having published any of his writings.[51]

---

50 Paul Oskar Kristeller, 'Between the Italian Renaissance and the French Enlightenment: Gabriel Naudé as an Editor', *Renaissance Quarterly*, 32(1) (Spring 1979): 41–72; especially pp. 55–58; Cavazza, 'Girolamo Rorario', p. 130N2.

51 Paschini, 'Un pordenonese', p. 211. On Rorario and Giberti see Paschini, 'Un pordenonese', p. 173 (quoting Rorario's letter to Giberti from Vienna, 31 July 1524). At that time Parmigianino was Giberti's protegé: see Giorgio Vasari, *Le vite de' piu eccellenti pittori, scultori ed architettori* in *Le opera*, VOL. 5, p. 22. See also Adriano

His *Dialogues*, inspired by Lucian, survived in manuscript form. A playful discourse, also inspired by Lucian, about a great number of mice inhabiting the gardens of Cardinal Campeggi, was published in 1648; *Quod animalia bruta* was published the same year. *Julius exclusus*, a pamphlet against Pope Julius II which was attributed at different times either to Erasmus or to Rorario, is probably by neither.[52]

Nothing in Rorario's writings suggests unorthodox attitudes, nothing that anticipated the thinking of seventeenth-century *libertins érudits* like Gabriel Naudé. 'In this case, as in many others, the editor was more important than the author': so wrote Paul Oskar Kristeller, in an article devoted to Naudé's editorial work on Italian texts.[53] In the same article, Kristeller mentioned a manuscript of Rorario's—*Quod animalia bruta*—at the Biblioteca Comunale of Siena, that differs from the one (now lost) Naudé used for his edition. In addition to some minor discrepancies, the manuscript now at Siena includes a passage highly critical of Francis I, king of France, that does not appear in any printed edition. Where the inflammatory passage would have occurred, Naudé inserted a series of asterisks; in other words, the editor acted as censor.[54] An alternative hypothesis, put forward by Silvano Cavazza,

---

Prosperi, *Tra evangelismo e controriforma: Gian Matteo Giberti (1495–1543)* (Rome: Edizioni di storia e letteratura, 2011).

52 Cavazza, 'Girolamo Rorario'.

53 Kristeller, 'Between the Italian Renaissance': 57.

54 Kristeller, 'Between the Italian Renaissance'. See Biblioteca Comunale di Siena, ms. H. IX. 6.

ascribes the suppression to Rorario himself: his decision to dedicate the dialogue he never published to Perrenot de Granvelle would have, in Cavazza's mind, necessitated the removal of a potentially offensive passage.[55] But Granvelle, a diplomat who spent a large part of his life in the service of Emperor Charles V, would have been utterly unmoved by Rorario's anti-French tirade.

8. As Cavazza convincingly argued, the Sienese manuscript preserves an earlier version of *Quod animalia bruta*, presumably the one Rorario sent to his correspondent Pietro Paolo Gualtieri.[56] Bayle's boundless curiosity and erudition, which granted Rorario a lasting fame, would have certainly hailed an edition of the Sienese manuscript, which hopefully will soon take place. But the impact of Rorario's text remains obscure. It touched a nerve—albeit belatedly. Why?

My tentative answer will start from *Pathosformeln*, 'formulas of emotion': a concept which Aby Warburg developed to explain the re-emergence in the art of the Renaissance of visual formulas from antiquity. In an earlier essay, I proposed the analogous idea of *Logosformeln*, 'formulas of reasoning'.[57] The recovery of ancient texts opened up conceptual possibilities and constraints, shaping the European encounter with old and new realities. Two examples will clarify my argument.

---

55 Cavazza, 'Girolamo Rorario': 157N57.

56 Cavazza, 'Girolamo Rorario': 157N56.

57 Carlo Ginzburg, *Wooden Eyes: Nine Reflections on Distance* (New York: Columbia University Press, 2001), p. 113.

The first deals with Pietro Pomponazzi, the Mantuan philosopher who, between 1489 and 1525, taught Aristotle's philosophy at the universities of Padua and Bologna. In an important article, Bruno Nardi analysed Pomponazzi's teaching, relying on a series of unpublished notes taken by his pupils.[58] In March 1523, in the middle of the lecture he was giving in Bologna on Aristotle's *De Meteoris*, Pomponazzi suddenly announced to his audience the extra-ordinary news he had just received from a friend. This was Antonio Pigafetta, the well-known traveller, who had sent to Isabel, queen of Portugal, a detailed account of three months he had spent journeying into the Southern Hemisphere. Pomponazzi had been surprised to learn that Pigafetta had encountered a large native population, since after all, according to Aristotle, no human being could live in those regions. Therefore, Pomponazzi told his students, Aristotle's words on this subject were 'rubbish' (*fatuitates*). On the day after this digression, Pomponazzi mentioned in his class a difficulty raised by some theologians. If those newly discovered populations were, like the people of the Northern Hemisphere, descendants of Adam, why did Christ not care about their salvation? This should be answered by the friars, Pomponazzi flippantly replied (*Ad hoc respondeo quod hoc solvant fratres*). But then said: if Aristotle and his commentator (Averroés) do not know what took

58 Bruno Nardi, 'I corsi manoscritti di lezioni e il ritratto di Pietro Pomponazzi' in *Studi su Pietro Pomponazzi* (Firenze: Felice Le Monnier, 1965), pp. 3–53; especially pp. 41–4.

place on earth, they could hardly know what happens in Heaven. And he concluded by suggesting that perhaps Christ had succeeded in being crucified in the Southern Hemisphere as well.

Among the students who attended Pomponazzi's lectures, according to Nardi, was Ercole Gonzaga, the son of Isabella d'Este.[59] The presence of Juan Ginés de Sepúlveda was perhaps more significant. Translator and commentator of Aristotle's Politics, Sepúlveda regarded American Indios as 'servants by nature': stupid, corrupt, barbarous people, hardly better than brutes. Even Mexican buildings, according to Sepúlveda, could not be regarded as evidence of human ingenuity, since bees and spiders build things no human can imitate.[60] In the same vein, a certain Gregorio had argued that Aristotle's theory concerning those who are slaves by nature 'is equitable, if applied to those who are by nature servants and barbarians: those who have neither insight nor understanding, like these Indios, whom everybody considers speaking beasts.'[61] In

59 Nardi, 'I corsi manoscritti', p. 43 (Ercole Gonzaga attended Pomponazzi's courses between 1522 and 1525).

60 Giuliano Gliozzi, *Adamo e il nuovo mondo* (Firenze: La Nuova Italia, 1977), p. 294 onwards; especially p. 295, quoting from Juan Ginés de Sepúlveda, *Democrates secundus sive de justis belli causis* (Angel Losada ed. and trans.) (Madrid: Instituto Francisco de Vitoria, 1951), p. 36. See also Aristotle, *De republica libri VIII* (Juan Ginés de Sepúlveda ed.) (for Philip, Prince of Spain) (Paris, 1548) (BUB: A. IV. N. I. 6; from Ulisse Aldrovandi's library).

61 Gliozzi, *Adamo*, p. 288 (quoting from Bartolome de las Casas, *Historia de las Indias*, p. 198).

a passage of his posthumously published dialogue *Democrates secundus*, Sepúlveda unfolded the chilling implications of this attitude. He compared the war against Indios to hunting wild animals: both activities, Sepúlveda commented, quoting Aristotle, were 'by nature just'.[62]

9. My second example deals with Plutarch and his most famous sixteenth-century reader, Michel de Montaigne. There are innumerable explicit references to Plutarch in Montaigne's *Essays*: I will quote a passage, from the *Apology for Raymond Sebond* which opens with an implicit nod to Plutarch but goes much beyond him:

> Why should it be a defect in the beasts not in us which stops all communication between us? We can only guess whose fault it is that we cannot understand each other: for we do not understand them any more than they understand us. They may reckon us to be brute beasts for the same reason that we reckon them to be so. It is no great miracle if we cannot understand them: we cannot understand Basques or Troglodytes![63]

---

62 Sepúlveda, *Democrates secundus sive de justis belli causis*.

63 Michel de Montaigne, *The Complete Essays* (M. A. Screech trans.) (London: Penguin Books, 1991), p. 506. See Michel de Montaigne, *Essais* (Albert Thibaudet ed.) (Paris: Gallimard, 1950), p. 498: 'Ce defaut qui empesche la communication d'entre elles et nous, pourquoy n'est il aussi bien à nous qu'à elles? C'est à deviner, à qui est la faute de ne nous entendre point: car nous ne les entendons non plus qu'elles nous. Par cette mesme raison, elles nous peuvent estimer bestes, comme nous les en

By a stunning reversal, humans were suddenly considered through the eyes of brutes. Language ceased to be the sign of an irreducible difference between humans and beasts; rather, it became the sign of a bridgeable difference. One can try to learn the Basque language; one can even make an effort to understand Brazilian cannibals.[64] In the case of Montaigne, Plutarch's open attitude towards beasts coexisted with (and possibly inspired) an open attitude towards humans. We are at the very opposite of Gregorio's Aristotelian definition of the Indios as 'talking beasts'.

10. But I am not opposing Plutarch to Aristotle on this subject. As we have seen, Plutarch's approach to the intelligence of brutes developed arguments put forward by Aristotle. Moreover, Plutarch's emphatic statement, which he supported by the authority of Empedocles and Heraclitus, that 'man is not altogether innocent of injustice when he treats animals [*ta zoa*] as he does',[65] may have been inspired by a passage on natural law in Aristotle's *Rhetoric* that also includes a reference to Empedocles, who said:

> in regard to not killing that which has life, for this is not right for some and wrong for others,

estimons. Ce n'est pas grand' merveille si nous ne les entendons pas; aussi ne faisons nous les Basques et les Troglodites.'

64 Carlo Ginzburg, 'Montaigne, Cannibals and Grottoes', *History and Anthropology* 6(2–3) (1993): 125–55.

65 Plutarch, *Moralia* 964 D.

> *But a universal precept, which extends without a break through-out the wide-ruling sky and the boundless earth.*[66]

We could rephrase these words by saying that the symbolic association between beasts and innocence is a transcultural phenomenon, not unconnected to the idea, put forward by some religions, that humans are intrinsically guilty. The supreme innocence conveyed by the comparison of the Servant of God to a lamb, in Isaiah—'He was oppressed, and he was afflicted, yet he opened not his mouth; he is brought as a lamb to the slaughter [. . .]'[67]—turned into the supreme innocence of Jesus the lamb.

We are apparently far away from the soul of brutes. But a closer look at Bayle's article 'Rorarius' suggests a different conclusion. I will mention only one aspect of Bayle's deliberately tortuous strategy. He arrayed all the authors who had argued for the intelligence of brutes, from Girolamo Rorario onwards, against Descartes and his theory of *animaux-machines*, beasts as automata. Bayle made no attempt to analyse the Cartesian theory according to its own principles, as a rigorous consequence of the opposition between mind and matter, *res cogitans* and *res extensa*. Instead he presented the theory in a fashion that made it appear quite absurd; then stubbornly pretended to defend it as a theory that was not only useful, but indispensable to Christian theologians. If, contrary to Descartes's argument, beasts were not automata, their suffering

66 Aristotle, *Art of Rhetoric* (J. H. Freese trans.) (Cambridge, MA: Harvard University Press, 1926, Loeb Classical Library 193), 1.13 [emphasis added].

67 Isa. 53:7.

would be unacceptable. Human suffering is different—it has been brought about by Adam's sin. But what about the beasts? Can we attribute to God the suffering of innocent beasts?[68]

Bayle's painful reflections on divine justice—or the lack of it—were elicited by the pain of brutes. This is not the exception but the rule. We speak of them, we think of us.

---

68 Bayle, *Dictionnaire historique et critique*, VOL. 4, p. 77nC.

Calvino, Manzoni and the Gray Zone[1]

1. First of all, there is a memory, an image. It is summer. Dusk. Primo Levi and Italo Calvino are talking animatedly (Calvino is taller) and walking down the road towards the village of Rhêmes Notre-Dame. It was at Rhêmes, a little side valley of the Aosta Valley, that the co-workers and friends of the Einaudi publishing house used to meet each summer. The discussions would go on for about a week.[2] That was the only year that Primo Levi attended, at least at the same time as I—it must have been 1980 or 1981. The meaning of that image imprinted in my memory became evident in retrospect when Sergio Solmi's translation into Italian of Raymond Queneau's *Petite cosmogonie portative* was published by Einaudi in 1982. Calvino wrote

1 Originally published in French as 'Levi, Calvino et la zone grise' at the international conference 'Primo Levi. L'homme, le témoin, l'écrivain', Paris, 11 April 2012. Later published as the Foreword in Primo Levi, *La zone grise: entretien avec Anna Bravo et Federico Cereja* (Paris: Payot and Rivages, 2014).

2 For a warm remembrance of these get-togethers, see Ernesto Ferrero, *Rhêmes o della felicità* (Turin: Liaison, 2008).

an Afterword for it, entitled 'Piccola guida alla Piccola Cosmogonia' (Little Guide to the Little Cosmogony), where he thanked Levi, 'who with his professional knowledge as a chemist and the agility of his sense of humour managed to get a handle on many of the passages that had remained inaccessible to me.'[3] In an enthusiastic review dedicated to the *Petite cosmogonie portative*, Levi referred to Calvino's 'Piccola guida' as 'very sharp'.[4] In 1986, he recalled the work he did on Queneau 'with happiness and amusement' at Rhêmes Notre-Dame as the 'happiest hour' of his friendship with Calvino, who had died the year before.[5]

The chemist who had helped Calvino decipher Queneau's arcane allusions to Mendeleev's periodic table was also the author of *The Periodic Table*, that very fine book where the table of the elements

---

3 Raymond Queneau, *Piccola cosmogonia portatile* (Sergio Solmi trans.) (Turin: Einaudi, 1982); Italo Calvino, 'Piccola Guida alla Piccola Cosmogonia' [Afterword] in Queneau, *Piccola cosmogonia portatile*, p. 162; Raymond Queneau, *Petite cosmogonie portative* (Paris: Gallimard, 1950). Calvino worked on it between 1978 and 1981: see the note in Italo Calvino, *Romanzi e racconti*, VOL. 1 (Mario Barenghi and Bruno Falcetto eds) (Milan: Arnoldo Mondadori Editore, 1991), p. *lxxxiv*. For the correspondence between Levi and Calvino about *Petite cosmogonie portative*, see Italo Calvino, *Italo Calvino: Letters, 1941–1985* (Martin McLaughlin trans.) (Princeton, NJ: Princeton University Press, 2013), p. 532 [Letter dated 30 April 1985].

4 Primo Levi, *L'altrui mestiere* (Turin: Einaudi, 1985), pp. 150–4, especially p. 153.

5 Primo Levi, 'Calvino, Queneau e le scienze', in *Opere*, VOL. 2 (Marco Belpoliti ed.) (Turin: Einaudi, 1997), pp. 1344–6. See Gabriella Poli and Giorgio Calcagno, *Echi di una voce perduta* (Milan: Mursia, 1992), pp. 329–31. For Levi's comment in response to a request from Calvino in relation to his translation of Queneau's *Le chant du Styrène*, see Calvino, *Letters* [Letter dated 10 August 1985].

was used as a metaphor for the various and sundry way of impersonating the human condition.[6] However, can we really detect a non-metaphoric equivalent of Mendeleev's table in the sphere of human relationships? In his exploration of the 'transversal bonds which link the world of nature to that of culture', Levi implicitly asked this kind of question and sought an answer.[7]

2. The *Personal Anthology* that Levi entitled *The Search for Roots* starts with Job. 'Why start with Job?' Levi asks. He answers:

> because this magnificent and harrowing story encapsulates the questions of all the ages, those for which man has never to this day found an answer, nor will we ever find one, but he will always search for it because he needs it in order to live, to understand himself and the world. Job is the just man oppressed by injustice.[8]

---

6 'Moreover, there is an immense patrimony of metaphors that the writer can take from the chemistry of today and yesterday': Primo Levi, 'Ex-Chemist' in *Other People's Trades* (Raymond Rosenthal trans.) (London: Abacus, 1991), p. 175. See Primo Levi, *The Periodic Table* (Raymond Rosenthal trans.) (New York: Penguin, 2000): 'Sandro seemed to be made of iron, and he was bound to iron by an ancient kinship' (p. 36); 'more obscurely, he felt the need to prepare himself (and to prepare me) for an iron future' (p. 37). Therefore, Calvino's comment needs to be corrected when he wrote that 'Argon' was the only chapter in *The Periodic Table* where an element is a metaphor; see Italo Calvino, *I libri degli altri* (Giovanni Tesio ed.) (Turin: Einaudi, 1991), p. 606 [Letter dated 12 October 1974].

7 Levi, *Trades*, p. *viii*.

8 Primo Levi, *The Search for Roots: A Personal Anthology* (Chicago: Ivan R. Dee, 2001), p. 11.

Job is 'man' in general. However, in this phrase, we can hear an autobiographical timbre, which becomes clear a few lines later when Levi says that Job, the just, is 'degraded to an animal for an experiment' by the wager between Satan and God. In a passage of *If This Is a Man* that was to become famous, Levi had talked of Auschwitz as an experiment:

> a gigantic biological and social experiment. Thousands of individuals, differing in age, condition, origin, language, culture and customs, are enclosed within barbed wire: there they live a regular, controlled life which is identical for all and inadequate to all needs, and which is more rigorous than any experimenter could have set up to establish what is essential and what is adventitious to the conduct of the human animal in the struggle for life.[9]

---

9 Primo Levi, '*If This Is a Man' and 'The Truce'* (Stuart Woolf trans.) (London: Abacus, 2002), p. 93. See Daniele Del Giudice's introduction to the Italian original with his seconding of Claude Lévi-Strauss's definition of Levi as a 'great ethnographer' in Primo Levi *Opere*, VOL. 1 (Marco Belpoliti ed.) (Turin: Einaudi, 1977), p. *lxii*. Levi writes again about 'the experimental character of the camps' in Primo Levi, 'Arbeit Macht Frei (1959)' in *The Black Hole of Auschwitz* (Sharon Wood trans.) (Malden, MA: Polity, 2005), p. 8. See Massimo Bucciantini, *Esperimento Auschwitz: Auschwitz Experiment* (Turin: Einaudi, 2011).

As Calvino immediately noted, Job evokes Auschwitz.[10] However, several years had already passed since Levi began to ask himself whether the dichotomy, embodied by Job, between the just man and injustice, had been, even at Auschwitz, always clear cut. 'There are a number of signs to suggest that the time has come to explore the space that separates the victims from the executioners, and to do it with a lighter touch and a less equivocal spirit than has been done, for example in some well-known recent films,' he wrote in his preface to *The Night of the Girondins*, the story by Jacob Presser that he translated.[11] In a 1979 interview, Levi talked of a project that was to involve 'taking a stand in the face of ambiguity'.[12] In another 1979 interview, he explains that he wanted to re-examine his experiences in the concentration camp: 'After all the polemic about the identification between victim and oppressor, the theme of guilt, the extreme ambiguity of that place, the grey band that separated the oppressed from the oppressors'.[13]

---

10 'I would suggest that it was the very presence of the Book of Job as an introduction to this "search for roots" that reminds us that the journey of Primo Levi passed through Auschwitz.' See Italo Calvino, Review, *La Repubblica* (11 July 1981); now available as Calvino, Afterword in Levi, *Search for Roots*, p. 222.

11 Primo Levi, 'Preface to Presser's *The Night of the Girondins*' in *Black Hole*, p. 36. The reference is to Liliana Cavani's film *The Night Porter* (1974).

12 Primo Levi, *Conversazioni e interviste: 1963–1987* (Marco Belpoliti ed.) (Turin: Einaudi, 1997), p. 158 [Interview with G. Arian Levi, originally published in *Ha Keillah*, February 1979].

13 Primo Levi, *The Voice of Memory: Interviews, 1961–1987* (Marco Belpoliti and David Gordon eds) (New York: Polity, 2000), p. 131.

This is the announcement of 'The Gray Zone', an extremely dense chapter of Levi's last book, *The Drowned and the Saved.* However, the topic (not the metaphor) was already there in his first book, *If This Is a Man*, in the chapter titled 'The Drowned and the Saved'.[14] After the passing of almost 40 years, the title of this chapter became the title of a book, one which closed his literary journey (and, a little later, his life). However, the tones of the two texts are extremely different. The chapter was written by a witness who is remembering; the chapter of *The Drowned and the Saved* by a witness who is reflecting. The distance in time between the events is reinforced by a literary filter, *The Betrothed*, which was already on Levi's mind at the time of his 1979 interview:

> when Renzo Tramaglino threatens don Abbondio with a knife. Manzoni observes that the oppressor, don Rodrigo, is also responsible for the minor acts of oppression carried out by his victims. It is a theme I recognize all too well. It is a stupid mistake to see all the demons on one side and all the saints on the other. It wasn't like that at all [. . .] To divide into black and white means not to know human nature.[15]

---

14 Primo Levi, *The Drowned and the Saved* (Raymond Rosenthal trans.) (New York: Vintage, 1989); Levi, *If This Is a Man*, pp. 93–106. In an earlier draft, 'The Drowned and the Saved' was the title of Chapter 2, which then became 'On the Bottom': see Philippe Mesnard, *Primo Levi: Le passage d'un témoin* (Paris: Fayard, 2011), p. 188.

15 Primo Levi, 'A Conversation with Primo Levi (1979)', interview by Giuseppe Grassano in *Voice of Memory*, pp. 121–35, especially pp. 131–2.

Direct and indirect echoes of *The Betrothed* appear very often in Levi's writings and interviews. In fact, this passage from Alessandro Manzoni, which was evoked in an interview from 1979 and then quoted in 'The Gray Zone', the chapter in *The Drowned and the Saved*, is especially important. Levi chose Manzoni as a guide for advancing towards the slippery slopes of 'ambiguity', towards a topic rooted in the experience he went through at Auschwitz. Why Manzoni?

3. For the young Levi, 'the chemistry and the physics on which we fed [. . .] were the antidote to Fascism.' As we read in the chapter 'Iron' in *The Periodic Table*:

> Professor D handed each of us precisely one gram of a certain powder: by the next day we had to complete the qualitative analysis, that is, to report what metals and non-metals it contained. Report in writing, like a police report, only yes and no, because doubts and hesitations were not admissible: it was each time a choice, a deliberation, a mature and responsible undertaking, for which Fascism had not prepared us, and from which emanated a good smell, dry and clean.[16]

The periodic table of elements demands clear answers: 'the chemist's trade consists in good part in being aware of these differences [like those between sodium and potassium, which are almost the same] [. . .] And not only the chemist's trade,' as Levi

16 Levi, *Table*, pp. 31–2, 39–40.

summed it up in 1975.[17] However, Levi's conviction that the clear answers of the world of chemistry could be extended to the human sphere was destined to break down a little later, corroded by his incessant reflections on the experience of Auschwitz. '[T]he newcomers to the Lager, whether young or not'[18] had immediately learnt that there was an ambiguous zone between the oppression and the oppressed, inhabited by the privileged oppressed, who collaborated with the oppressor to greater or lesser degrees. Ambiguity is not difference. (There are no ambiguities in the periodic table of elements.) The oppressed person who oppresses is an ambiguous being, an oxymoron: '[almost certainly] the dominant stylistic device, quantitatively and qualitatively, in Levi's works', as Pier Vincenzo Mengaldo demonstrated in a brilliant way, also evoking the gray zone.[19]

In 1976, Levi asked: 'Can Cohn be judged?' Cohn is a character in Presser's *The Night of the Girondins*, the Jew who does the Nazi's bidding by setting up the deportations to Sobibór. 'Well, the sense of the book is that Cohn *can* be judged.'[20] Ten years later, in *The Drowned and the Saved*, he reflected on the real people who

---

17 Levi, *Table*, p. 51. This passage is quoted from a different point of view by Cesare Cases, 'L'ordine delle cose e l'ordine delle parole' in Ernesto Ferrero (ed.), *Primo Levi: un'antologia della critica* (Turin: Einaudi, 1997), p. 7.
18 Levi, *Drowned*, p. 33.
19 Pierre Vicenzo Mengaldo, 'Lingua e scrittura in Levi' in *Per Primo Levi* (Turin: Einaudi, 2019), pp. 233–42; for the reference to the gray zone, see p. 238.
20 Levi, Preface to Presser, *The Night of the Girondins*', pp. 35–6.

collaborated with the Nazis and gave a different answer: 'it is necessary to declare the imprudence of issuing hasty moral judgment on such human cases.'[21] In a strategic position, he inserts a quotation from *The Betrothed*, which he had alluded to in an interview some years before:

> Alessandro Manzoni, the nineteenth-century novelist and poet, knew this quite well: 'Provocateurs, oppressors, all those who in some way injure others, are guilty not only of the evil they commit but also of the perversion into which they lead the spirit of the offended.' The condition of the offended does not exclude culpability, which is often objectively serious, but I know of no human tribunal to which one could delegate the judgment.[22]

'I know of no human tribunal': the person who wrote these words did not know any other kind of tribunal, but these words show how dense the mental dialogue was between Levi, an atheist, and Manzoni, a Catholic convert who did recognize divine judgement as the decisive appeal. Nevertheless, in this mental dialogue, there is the phrase 'on such human cases' which should be associated with casuistry, i.e. the perspective that aims to verify concretely, through the analysis of specific cases, the abstract formulations of laws and moral laws. This connection with casuistry is confirmed by Levi's

---

21 Levi, *Drowned*, p. 44.

22 Levi, *Drowned*, pp.43–4.

use of the technical expression 'cases of conscience' in his preface to a book in which Hermann Langbein (another Auschwitz inmate) had minutely analysed the concentration-camp system 'down to the grey band of the Kapos and the prisoners with privileged status'.[23]

4. I started out with a very broad definition of casuistry, which I will try to specify historically. Manzoni, who had converted to an austere Catholicism inspired by Jansenism, was an enthusiastic reader of the Port-Royal writers. He always had a negative bias towards casuistry.[24] This can be seen in *A Vindication of Catholic Morality* (1819), which Manzoni wrote on the prompting of Monsignor Luigi Tosi, in response to the last chapter of Sismondi's *Histoire des républiques italiennes* (1818).[25] Sismondi attributed most of the moral decadence of the Italians to the Catholic Church, and especially to the corrupting effects of casuistry. Manzoni answered

---

23 Primo Levi, 'Preface to H. Langbein's *People in Auschwitz*' in *Black Hole*, p. 81. Levi had already referred to Langbein's book which had not yet been translated into Italian, in his Preface to Presser's *The Night of the Girondins*'. In Langbein's chapter, 'Jewish VIPs', Langbein notes that Primo Levi himself, in *If This Is a Man*, realized that he did not investigate the hierarchy that ruled the camp enough (Hermann Langbein, *People in Auschwitz* (Harry Zohn trans.) (Chapel Hill: University of North Carolina Press, 2004), pp. 169ff. Levi calls Langbein 'a dear friend of mine, a person I highly respect', see Risa Sodi, 'An Interview with Primo Levi', *Partisan Review* 54(3) (1987): 364.

24 On all this, see the still fundamental book, Francesco Ruffini, *La vita religiosa di Alessandro Manzoni*, 2 VOLS (Bari: G. Laterza, 1931).

25 Jean Charles Léonard de Sismondi, *Histoire des républiques italiennes du Moyen Age*, VOL. 16 (Paris: Treuttel et Wurtz, 1818), pp. 407–60.

this accusation by defending Catholic morality, but he did this distancing himself from the casuists. He stated that he had read 'not even one of them' and that he knew them only through 'the confutation and censure directed against many of them' (first of all, certainly, by Pascal in *Provinciales*).[26] Perhaps Manzoni's flat-out statement is not entirely true, but its substantial point, which takes us back to Levi and the gray zone, is another one. When people discuss casuistry, they often mix up two elements—the analysis of situations and the judgment that derives from it. Moral laxity, frequent in casuistry, above all Jesuit casuistry, is not a necessary consequence of it. Sismondi himself recognized this. In a letter to the Unitarian theologian William Ellery Channing from 1833, he wrote:

> Those who believe that morality consists in only several simple precepts that are quickly wiped away seem to me to be very superficial observers. On the contrary, the more we study, the more we see the field broaden. One could convince oneself of this by reading the thousands of books written on cases of conscience in the Catholic church. The secret of the confessional, the need finally to agree on an absolution and maintain priestly power—these things certainly made the casuists deviate and create, through their help, what one had termed Jesuit morality. Nevertheless,

26 Sismondi, p. 413ff; Alessandro Manzoni, *A Vindication of Catholic Morality* (London: Keating and Brown, 1836), pp. 61–5.

> great progress has been made by them in this noble science and perhaps we owe more to them than to the Bible itself for the establishment of the system of Christian morality.[27]

Manzoni's rigorist morality prevented him from arriving at a conclusion like this. However, in his novel, the subtle distinctions that he makes in the moral sphere, rather than mitigating the severity of the judgment, make his judgment more precise. Thus, in the passage from *The Betrothed* that Levi quoted in relation to the 'gray zone', the perversion of the oppressed by the oppressors compounds the judgment against the oppressors. This passage is tacitly re-echoed by Levi a little bit before the conclusion of 'The Gray Zone': 'an infernal order such a National Socialism exercises a frightful power of corruption, against which it is difficult to guard oneself. It degrades its victims and makes them similar to itself, because it needs both great and small complicities.'[28]

The Special Squads present us with an extreme case—the Sonderkommandos who were assigned to the management of the crematoriums. 'Conceiving and organizing the squads was National Socialism's most demonic crime.' Yet, Levi cautions us: 'Therefore I ask that we meditate on the story of "the crematorium ravens" with pity and rigor, but that judgment of them be suspended.'[29] Nevertheless, to abstain from judgement on the oppressed who have become

27 Ruffini, *La vita religiosa*, VOL. 2, pp. 182–3.

28 Levi, *Drowned*, p. 68

29 Levi, *Drowned*, p. 60.

accomplices in oppression is something that is very different from absolving or pardoning the oppressors. 'To forgive is not my verb,' Levi said in an interview. 'I am not a believer, the phrase "I absolve thee", has no precise meaning for me. I don't believe that anyone, not even a priest, has the power to bind and release others.'[30] In another interview, in referring to a Jewish rather than Christian context, he said, 'Since I'm not a believer, I really don't know what forgiveness is. It's a concept that's outside my world. I don't have the authority to bestow forgiveness. If I would be a rabbi, maybe I would have it; even if I would be a judge, maybe.'[31] Therefore, rejecting the false equivalence suggested by the statement '*tout comprendre c'est tout pardonner*', Levi resolutely distances himself from the second term [*pardonner*] and opts for the first [*comprendre*]. 'I would like to understand you to judge you,' he wrote to his German translator, addressing himself to his German readers.[32] In fact, he wanted to try to understand how Auschwitz had been possible and to understand 'also in a broader sense, because I would like to understand something else: as a chemist, I want to understand the world around me.'[33] However, as we have seen, in the face

---

30 Primo Levi, '*The Drowned and the Saved* (1986)', interview by Giorgio Calcagno, in *Voice of Memory*, pp. 109–13; here, pp. 109–10. Originally entitled/published as Primo Levi, 'Capire non è perdonare' [Understanding is not Pardoning], *La Stampa* (26 July 1986).

31 Sodi, 'An Interview with Primo Levi': 362.

32 Levi, *Opere*, VOL. 2, p. 1129.

33 Levi, 'Interview with Giorgio Calcagno', p. 111.

of the ambiguities of Auschwitz, chemistry, with its clear classifications, is disarmed. What does emerge here is the profound debt of Primo Levi, a 'Jewish Italian', as he wished to define himself, to Alessandro Manzoni, a Catholic convert—and, more precisely, to a Manzoni who was paradoxically close to casuistry.[34]

5. How can we explain this debt, this contiguity? I think the answer should be sought in the crossings, not yet studied adequately, between the Talmud and Christian casuistry. Levi dedicated an article entitled 'Ritual and Laughter' to a compendium of Talmudic wisdom provided by *The Set Table*, the famous book by Joseph ben Ephraim Karo printed in Venice in 1565, which he read in translation. Levi first lists in an amused tone several of the ritual distinctions that Karo analysed with extremely minute casuistic subtlety and then takes flight towards the cosmos:

> Behind these curious pages I perceive an ancient taste for bold discussion, an intellectual flexibility that does not fear contradictions, indeed welcomes them as an inevitable ingredient of life; and life is rule, it is order prevailing over Chaos, but the rule has crevices, unexplored pockets of exception, license, indulgence and disorder. Trouble is in store for anyone who cancels them, perhaps they contain

34 Marco Belpoliti, *Primo Levi* (Milan: Mondadori, 1998), pp. 111–14. Available in English translation as *Primo Levi: An Identikit* (Clarissa Botsford trans.) (London: Seagull Books, 2022).

> the germ of all our tomorrows, because the machine of the universe is subtle, subtle are the laws which rule it, and every year the rules obeyed by sub-atomic particles reveal themselves to be more and more subtle. Einstein's words have often been quoted: 'The Lord is subtle, but he is not wicked'; hence subtle must be, in His likeness, those who follow Him. One notes that among physicists and cyberneticists there are many Jews from Eastern Europe: could their *esprit de finesse* be a Talmudic inheritance?[35]

It is a cheerful page where we come across the 'agility of his [Levi's] sense of humor', the same agility that Calvino admiringly wrote about when he remembered their work together on the *Petite cosmogonie portative*. Nevertheless, it is cheer that is ambiguous, illusory. Behind the praise of the exception as the 'germ of all our tomorrows', we perceive casuistry, *esprit de finesse*, subtlety—the instruments with which Primo Levi was to face his terrible yesterday, the ambiguities of the gray zone.

35 Levi, 'Ritual and Laughter', *Trades*, pp. 196–200, especially pp. 199–200.

Schema and Bias

A HISTORIAN'S REFLECTION ON DOUBLE-BLIND EXPERIMENTS[1]

To Vittorio Foa

1. The life of a reader is full of surprises. One of these—a page of *Art and Illusion*, Ernst Gombrich's great book—will be the starting point of my reflections. From the very moment I came across that page, nearly 50 years ago, I received a strong impression which has stayed with me, under different forms, even today.

The page is included in the chapter 'Truth and the Stereotype'. Figure 1A (overleaf) is an engraving based on an English lithograph, dated 1836, representing the western facade of Notre-Dame Cathedral at Chartres. Figure 1B, a modern photograph of the same facade.[2] The

---

1 I received suggestions and help from Maria Luisa Catoni and Raffaele Piumelli. I remain grateful to both.

2 Figure 1A is now in the public domain; and Figure 1B is similar but not identical to the page in the Gombrich volume. For more information, please see the Image Credits.

FIGURE 1A (LEFT): Robert Garland, *Chartres Cathedral* (1836). Engraving after a lithograph from B. Winkles, *French Cathedrals* (London, 1837).

FIGURE 1B (RIGHT): Present-day photograph of Chartres Cathedral.

difference between the engraving and the photograph is evident. In the former, two rows of pointed Gothic arches; in the latter, two rows of round Romanesque arches. The author of the lithograph, impregnated with Romantic stereotypes, regarded French cathedrals as the emblem of the 'age of faith', embodied by the Gothic style: in his mental universe, Gombrich remarks, the Romanesque windows of the western facade had no place.[3]

Today, in the era of Photoshop, everybody is familiar with the idea that photographs can be manipulated in all possible ways. Let me immediately add that Gombrich had a predictably sophisticated attitude towards the objectivity of photographs. *Art and Illusion* begins by showing that photographs are also, in some way, constructed images: an issue Gombrich repeatedly analysed with great subtlety.[4] But a comparison with the photograph of Chartres Cathedral (and *a fortiori* a visual inspection of the cathedral itself) shows that the English lithographer, notwithstanding his concern to provide an architecturally accurate representation, had distorted reality—unless somebody would be able to demonstrate (to mention

---

3 E. H. Gombrich, *Art and Illusion: A Study in the Psychology of Pictorial Representation* (London: Phaidon Press, 1962[1960]), p. 63.

4 Gombrich, *Art and Illusion*, p. 30; E. H. Gombrich, 'Standards of Truth: The Arrested Image and the Moving Eye' in W. J. T. Mitchell (ed.), *The Language of Images* (Chicago: University of Chicago Press, 1980), pp. 181–217; E. H. Gombrich, 'Image and Code: Limits of Conventionalism in Pictorial Representation' in *The Image and the Eye: Further Studies in the Psychology of Pictorial Representation* (Oxford: Phaidon Press, 1982), pp. 278–97.

a completely absurd hypothesis) that the Romanesque arches on the western facade of Chartres Cathedral are the result of a restoration which took place after 1836.

Thus far, more or less, Gombrich. Now I venture to advance a corollary of his argument, extending the implications of the nineteenth-century lithograph of Chartres Cathedral to any kind of testimony—visual, verbal, whatever. Any testimony speaks, first of all, deliberately or not, of itself, of the ways in which it has been produced: in this case, of the Romantic stereotypes which inspired the lithographer. But it also speaks, in a more or less deliberate, more or less distorted way, of an outside reality (in this case, Chartres Cathedral). Those two sides are connected by a very tight relationship—one could compare them to two sides of a sheet of paper. To understand what a testimony can say about the world in which it has been produced, we should inscribe it in a series: for instance, the series based on nineteenth-century lithographs.[5] This would allow us to make a further step, exploring the relationship between that testimony and its referential dimension: the reality which it represents or pretends to represent.

A generalization based on a blatant case of image distortion—a lithograph inadvertently turning Romanesque arches into Gothic ones—might suggest a relativist conclusion. If we assume that all testimonies (including photographs) imply some kind of distortion,

---

5 See the French case analysed by Stephen Bann, *Parallel Lines: Printmakers, Painters and Photographers in Nineteenth-Century France* (New Haven, CT, and London: Yale University Press, 2001).

the boundary between true and false testimonies would disappear and Gombrich's appeal to the 'reality principle', mediated by the twentieth-century photograph of Chartres Cathedral, would become impossible. A similar objection has been raised against Gombrich by W. J. T. Mitchell, arguing for a 'hard, rigorous relativism that regards knowledge as a social product': an attitude very distant, he insisted, from 'some facile relativism that abandons "standards of truth" or the possibility of valid knowledge'.[6] But are rigorous relativists able to decide whether the representation of Gothic arches on the western facade of the Chartres Cathedral displayed in the English lithograph implies a distortion of reality?

This question (I am unable to say whether it is a rhetorical one) points out what is at stake in this debate: the meaning, no more no less, we ascribe to terms like 'knowledge', 'truth', 'reality'. Gombrich was so deeply aware of the general implications of the examples he analysed (including the one I mentioned) that as an epigraph for the chapter 'Truth and the Stereotype', he chose a passage on transcendental schematism taken from Kant's *Critique of Pure Reason*. The Kantian (although originally Greek) word 'schema' is at the very centre of Gombrich's comment on the English lithograph:

> Clearly, if we had pointed out to the artist his mistake, he could have further modified his scheme and rounded the windows [. . .]. [But] such matching will always be a step-by-step process—how long it takes and how hard it is will

6 W. J. T. Mitchell, *Iconology: Image, Text, Ideology* (Chicago: University of Chicago Press, 1986), pp. 37–9.

> depend on the choice of the initial schema to be adapted to the task of serving as a portrait. I believe that in this respect these humble documents do indeed tell us a lot about the procedure of any artist who wants to make a truthful record of an individual truth. He begins not with his visual impression but with his idea or concept [. . .].[7]

Throughout his book, Gombrich provides a compelling argument for dismantling the notion (which goes back to Ruskin) of the 'innocent eye'. His demonstration might be taken in a narrow sense, as if it would apply to images only, or even to the subset of images aiming to represent reality through pictorial illusion. But my aforementioned extension to any testimonies—visual, verbal, whatever—is, if I am not mistaken, implicit in Gombrich's argument. Let me quote a passage in which Gombrich uses, as a synonym for 'innocent eye' the word 'unbiased':

> the postulate of an unbiased eye demands the impossible. It is the business of the living organism to organize, for where there is life there is not only hope, as the proverb says, but also fears, guesses, expectations which sort and model the incoming messages, testing and transforming and testing again.[8]

7 Gombrich, *Art and Illusion*, p. 63. On the Greek origins of schema, see the very rich book by M. L. Catoni: *La comunicazione non verbale nella Grecia antica* (Turin: Bollati Boringhieri, 2008[2005]).

8 Gombrich, *Art and Illusion*, p. 251.

'Unbiased', 'guesses', 'testing and testing again': Gombrich describes the production of images in terms evoking scientific knowledge. This analogy does not aim to turn the scientist into an artist—rather the opposite. This is why Mitchell rejected Gombrich's alleged 'scientism', advocating the aforementioned 'rigorous relativism' he placed symbolically (and, in my view, problematically) under the sign of Feyerabend.[9] But Gombrich's hero is, rather, Leonardo: the artist-scientist *par excellence*.[10]

Through a sequence of trial and error, Gombrich argues, echoing Popper, the artist (or the scientist) is able to trace a distinction between schemata and biases, hypotheses and prejudices, discarding the latter and approaching the former in order to represent (or to know) reality. Here comes my question (the first in a series): can the analogy between artist and scientist put forward by Gombrich in the aforementioned anti-relativist perspective be extended to the historian as well?

2. According to a widespread notion, historians start from hypotheses which are tested on the basis of a careful reading of the evidence, and then discarded, or modified, or turned into more or less solid

9 Mitchell, *Iconology*, pp. 37–9. For the analogy between science and art, proposed by Feyerabend, see Carlo Ginzburg, *Occhiacci di legno: Nove riflessioni sulla distanza* (Milan: Feltrinelli, 1998), pp. 155–9.

10 Refer to the index of J. B. Trapp (ed.), *E. H. Gombrich: A Bibliography* (London: Phaidon Press, 2000). But the distinction between 'true proposition' (in science) and 'psychological effect' (in art), introduced in particular about Leonardo in Gombrich, 'Experiment and Experience in the Arts' in *Image and the Eye*, pp. 215–43 [E. H. Gombrich, *L'immagine e l'occhio* (Turin: Einaudi, 1985), pp. 268–9] is too hasty.

(although potentially revocable) conclusions. But this seemingly innocent description of the historian's craft conceals several difficulties, related above all to the stage of 'testing and testing again' (as Gombrich said). Is the historian's testing compatible with experiments? In his unfinished methodological reflections, published after his death, Marc Bloch raised this question, answering in the negative. Experiments are not allowed to historians. 'This impossibility,' Bloch wrote, 'embodies the great, irredeemable weakness of our research vis-à-vis the majority of natural sciences.'[11]

This drastic statement, which can be read in the first draft of Bloch's *Métier d'historien*, was followed by a series of distinctions and nuances which were expanded in the next draft of his work. Other disciplines, like history, achieve knowledge indirectly, through traces. But, Bloch remarked, 'it seems obvious that any human phenomenon beyond the minimum threshold of complexity cannot be deliberately reproduced or provoked.' Even experiments conducted in the domain of individual psychology would be impossible in the domain of collective psychology: 'One could not—one would not dare, even assuming that one could—deliberately unleash [that is, for a cognitive purpose] a panic or a movement based on religious phanaticism.'[12]

11 Marc Bloch, *Apologia della storia o mestiere di storico* (Turin: Einaudi, 1950), p. 201ff.

12 Marc Bloch, *Apologie pour l'histoire ou Métier d'historien* in *L'Histoire, la Guerre, la Résistance* (Paris: Gallimard, 1986), p. 88; Bloch, *Apologia della storia*, p. 45ff.

The implications of this remark went beyond psychology. Clearly, Bloch was also alluding to the economic and social phenomena which *Annales*, the journal he founded in 1929 along with Lucien Febvre, put at the very centre of the debates among historians.

3. The impossibility of conducting experiments, pointed out by Bloch as well as by innumerable historians after him, apparently sets up rigid limitations to the process of testing and testing again which Gombrich (and Popper before him) evoked.[13] Among recent attempts to overcome the obstacle, one may mention *Natural Experiments of History*, a collection of essays edited by Jared Diamond and James A. Robinson. One of those essays approaches the relationship between the collapse of the Ancien Régime and the birth of capitalism in the following terms:

> In the natural sciences the solution of a problem like this would be to conduct an experiment. For instance, we would ideally take a group of countries that were alike—say, all of them having a relatively backward institutional landscape—and abolish Ancien Régime institutions in a randomly chosen subset of these countries (the 'treatment' group) while leaving unchanged the institutions of the rest (the 'control' group). Then we could observe what happens

---

13 See, for example, Luciano Canfora, *Togliatti e i dilemmi della politica* (Bari: Laterza, 1989), p. 54.

to the relative prosperity of these two groups. In reality, of course, we are unable to conduct such an experiment.[14]

Since the past cannot be manipulated, the essay's authors point out, one must rely upon a 'natural experiment' based on comparison: an alternative already mentioned by Bloch.

Comparison is a fascinating topic, but I will not deal with it. I will rather try to explore an apparently blocked trajectory, comparing, through a series of successive approximations, not 'natural sciences' in general, but, more specifically, double-blind experiments in medical science. Hopefully, analogies and divergences emerging from this comparison will shed some light on the historian's craft from an unexpected point of view—justified, however, by the traditional exchanges between history and medicine: two forms of knowledge born in ancient Greece, which shared the term *historia*, enquiry, and a series of mutual interactions. Historians have often been inspired by a cognitive model based on semiotics, supported by a sustained reflection on the relationship between anomalies and norms, between cases and general rules.[15]

---

14 See James A. Robinson, Daron Acemoglu, Davide Cantoni and Simon Johnson, 'From Ancien Régime to Capitalism: The French Revolution as a Natural Experiment' in Jared Diamond and James A. Robinson (eds), *Natural Experiments of History* (Cambridge, MA: Belknap Press of Harvard University Press, 2010), pp. 221–56; here, pp. 224–5. And see the preface to *Natural Experiments of History*, p. 1: 'one cannot manipulate the past.'

15 Carlo Ginzburg, 'Spie: Radici di un paradigma indiziario' [1979] in *Miti, emblemi, spie: morfologia e storia* (Turin: Einaudi, 1984), pp. 158–209; Arnaldo Momigliano,

A double-blind experiment can be described as follows: a group of doctors, researchers and nurses is asked to administer a group of patients a drug whose effectiveness must be tested—as well as a *placebo*, an inert product, whose aspect is undistinguishable from the previous one. Their respective nature is ignored by the patients who have been randomly given each of them, as well as by doctors, researchers and nurses who administer them and keep a record of effects and variations. This randomized controlled trial (RCT) implies therefore a twofold blindness with one relevant exception: the person or persons conducting the experiment.[16]

The history of double-blind experiments is long and tortuous.[17] A concern for testing the effects of medications, as opposed to suggestion and self-suggestion, first emerged in polemical contexts: in the debate on Mesmerism at the end of the eighteenth century; in the debate about hypnosis one century later. Ultimately, the issue was taken up by mainstream medical science. In 1917, Torald Sollmann, the American pharmacologist, administered an inert product, or placebo, to a control group in order to test the effectiveness of a drug: an experiment he labelled 'blind test' in a two-page paper entitled 'The Crucial Test of Therapeutic Evidence'.[18] A few

---

'History between Medicine and Rhetoric' [1985] in *Ottavo contributo alla storia degli studi clasiici e del mondo antico* (Rome: Edizioni di storia e letteratura, 1987), pp. 13–25.

16 Anne Harrington (ed.), *The Placebo Effect: An Interdisciplinary Exploration* (Cambridge, MA: Harvard University Press, 2000[1997]).

17 See T. J. Kaptchuk, 'Intentional Ignorance: A History of Blind Assessment and Placebo Controls in Medicine', *Bulletin of the History of Medicine* 72 (1988): 389–433.

decades later, it was realized that keeping patients in the dark about the nature of the administered product was not enough; effects due to suggestion could be unwillingly conveyed even by those who administered the product. Hence the use of double-blind experiments; but they had to overcome stubborn resistances. For a long time, its implications, as well as the limits, nature and the very existence of the placebo effect, raised many doubts. In the last decades, the debate took a new turn due to the ongoing research on the placebo effect from a neurobiological perspective.[19]

I limit myself to elementary information due to my rather limited knowledge in this matter. I will tentatively consider the placebo effect as a model (i.e. a miniature, and extremely simplified, image) of some fundamental phenomena of human behaviour; moreover, I will look at double-blind experiments as a simplified model of the perspective from which historians approach, or could approach, those phenomena. (I would like to emphasize that these are mere hypotheses; what I am doing is an experiment over an experiment.)

---

18 Torald Sollmann, 'The Crucial Test of Therapeutic Evidence', *Journal of American Medical Association* 69 (1917): 198–9; Arthur K. Shapiro, 'A Contribution to a History of the Placebo Effect', *Behavioral Science* 5 (1960): 109–35.

19 Arthur K. Shapiro and Elaine Shapiro, 'The Placebo: Is It Much Ado About Nothing?' in Harrington (ed.), *Placebo Effect*, pp. 12–36. For an updated bibliography, see Wikipedia on 'Placebo' (last accessed 11 March 2022). See especially Fabrizio Benedetti et al., 'Neurobiological Mechanisms of the Placebo Effect', *The Journal of Neuroscience* (9 November 2005): 10390–402 (brought to my attention by Maria Luisa Catoni).

This twofold, hypothetical analogy is based on four elements:

(a) the objects of double-blind experiments are individuals belonging to different animal species (including our own);

(b) those individuals experience emotions (fears, expectations, and so forth) which can have an impact on the experiment's results;

(c) those emotions can be experienced not only by patients but also by researchers involved in the experiment;

(d) in order to protect the outcome of the experiment, both the patients' and the researchers' emotions must be neutralized, by keeping both of them in the dark as far as the experiment is concerned.

How is all this related to history and historical research? The answer must be looked for, first of all, within the *placebo* effect, as well as within the opposite phenomenon which has been labelled the '*nocebo* effect': i.e. phenomena of suggestion and autosuggestion elicited, respectively, by hopes and fears (in some cases, the latter, according to a much-debated hypothesis, could bring a person to death).[20] The discovery of how suggestion and autosuggestion can affect human behaviour is inscribed in a long trajectory which, in our tradition, begins with the ruthless attack against religion and its psychological roots, launched by Epicurus and his followers—first of all, Lucretius. *Primus in orbe deos fecit timor*, 'fear first created

---

20 R. A. Hahn, 'The Nocebo Phenomenon: Scope and Foundations' in Harrington (ed.), *Placebo Effect*, pp. 56–76.

gods in the world': this line by Petronius must be read along with Tacitus' profound remark, *fingunt simul creduntque*: 'they create and at the same time believe in what they have created.'[21] Religions, a human creation, are born from fear and generate fear, are born from pain and soothe pain. The catchy title of a book written by two specialists, Arthur and Elaine Shapiro, and addressed to a large audience, points at this long trajectory: *The Powerful Placebo: from Ancient Priest to Modern Physician.*[22]

To identify religions with the placebo (or *timebo*) effect would be grotesque. Any conjecture on the origins of religions does not explain the meaning they acquired in societies as diverse as possible: unintended consequences are, as always in human history, the norm. But the miniature, simplified model based on double-blind experiments may shed a retrospective light on a critical tradition based on a ferocious demystification of the psychological roots of religion, along with a full recognition of its extraordinary effectiveness. The mannequins displayed in Hogarth's etching entitled *Some Principal Inhabitants of the Moon: Royalty, Episcopacy and Law* (1724) embody and perform ecclesiastical and secular power not *although* they are empty but *because* they are empty (see Figure 2). Goya, possibly inspired, either directly or indirectly, by Hogarth's

21 Carlo Ginzburg, *Paura reverenza terrore: Rileggere Hobbes oggi* (Parma: Monte Universita Parma, 2008). [Available in English as: *Fear Reverence Terror* (London: Seagull Books, 2017.)]

22 Arthur K. Shapiro and Elaine Shapiro, *The Powerful Placebo: From Ancient Priest to Modern Physician* (Baltimore: Johns Hopkins University Press, 1997).

FIGURE 2: *Some Principal Inhabitants of the Moon: Royalty, Episcopacy and Law* (1724) by William Hogarth.

FIGURE 3 (LEFT): Francisco de Goya, *Caprichos No. 52: 'Lo que puede un Sastre!'*

FIGURE 4 (RIGHT): Preparatory drawing by Francisco de Goya for *Caprichos No. 52.*

etching, represented in one of his *Caprichos* a woman kneeling at the feet of a monk's frock hanging from a tree (see Figure 3). In the preparatory drawing, the face inside the frock is erased (see Figure 4); in the etching, the sinister grimace of a mannequin emerges. In both versions, the frock is empty. 'Lo que puede un sastre!'—'What a tailor can do!' the caption reads.[23]

4. So far, I have been dealing with the placebo effect and its historical implications. The double-blind experiment, aiming to weaken the placebo effect, may be connected to a different sphere—that of historical research. From *res gestae* we shift to *historia rerum gestarum*. It would be tempting to regard the expectations nourished by patients and doctors, being kept in the dark to avoid interferences with the strategy of those who conduct the experiment, as an equivalent of the bias or romantic prejudice which, in the English lithograph analysed by Gombrich, turned the Romanesque arches of the western facade of Chartres Cathedral into Gothic arches. But from this hypothetical analogy a crucial divergence immediately

---

23 See Francis D. Klingender, *Goya in the Democratic Tradition* (New York: Sidgwick & Jackson, 1968[1948]), pp. 96–7. On p. 97n1, Klingender notes the iconographic similarity between Goya's drawing and the title page of a pamphlet that appeared in London in 1765: *Mumbo Chumbo: A Tale Written in the Antient Manner, Recommended to Modern Devotees.* On p. 178, Klingender mentions, in another context, the Hogarth print (of which he gives a reproduction). See Richard C. Trexler, 'Dressing and Undressing Images: An Analytic Sketch' in *Religion in Social Context in Europe and America, 1200–1700* (Tempe: Arizona Center for Medieval and Renaissance Studies, 2002), pp. 374–408.

emerges. In the double-blind experiment, the expectations nourished by doctors and patients must be analysed—but only as a disturbance, comparable to a background noise which must be weakened as much as possible. The historian's work, if inspired by a concern for testing the evidence, is, as we will see, completely different. I will approach this issue from a circumscribed point of view, which points to the direction which Bloch declared closed for ever: to conduct experiments in the domain of history.

5. In his book *Diritto e ragione: Teoria del garantismo penale* (Law and Reason. Protection of Civil Liberties in a Theoretical Perspective), Luigi Ferrajoli wrote:

> A trial is, in a certain sense, the only case of a 'historiographic experiment': testimonies are asked to act *de vivo*, since they are not only summoned directly, but also compared, submitted to cross-examinations and asked to re-enact, like in a psychodrama, the events which are at the centre of the trial.[24]

---

24 Luigi Ferrajoli, *Diritto e ragione: Teoria del garantismo penale* (Bari: Laterza, 1989), p. 32: 'Il processo è per così dire il solo caso di "esperimento storiografico": in esso le fonti sono fatte giocare *de vivo*, non solo perché sono assunte direttamente, ma anche perché sono messe a confronto tra loro, sottoposte ad esami incrociati e sollecitate a riprodurre, come in uno psicodramma, la vicenda giudicata.' I have quoted this passage in my *Il giudice e lo storico* (Turin: Einaudi, 1991), p. 14.

Nearly two centuries before, Volney, addressing himself to the pupils of École Normale in the third year of the Revolution, proclaimed:

> History is nothing other than a genuine enquiry on facts [*enquête*, i.e. *historia*]. The historian who is aware of his task must regard himself as a judge who summons those who either narrated or witnessed the facts, submitting them to cross-examination, interrogating them, trying to find truth.'[25]

The analogy between historian and judge is an old one, but Ferrajoli gave a new twist to it by connecting it to experiment. Being a jurist, he referred to trials in the making. Historians may work on court records which were produced centuries ago. In those cases, developing Ferrajoli's suggestion, we might speak of a 'historiographic experiment raised to the square': testimonies are asked to act *de vivo*, in the present, by the judge; later, they will be re-examined

25 'L'histoire n'est qu'une véritable enquête de faits. L'historien qui a le sentiment de ses devoirs dois se regarder comme un juge qui appelle devant lui les narrateurs et les témoins des faits, les confronte, les questionne et tâche d'arriver à la vérité'—Constantin-Francois de Chasseboeuf Volney, *Leçons d'histoire prononcées à l'École normale, en l'an III de la République française* (Paris: J.A. Brosson, 1826[1799]). I warmly thank Tami Sarfatti, to whom I owe this quote. And see Marc Bloch, 'Pour une histoire comparée des sociétés européennes' in *Mélanges historiques* (Charles-Edmond Perrin ed.) (Paris: Service d' Edition et de Vente des Publications de l'Education, 1963), pp. 16–40. (Bloch, *L'Histoire, la Guerre, la Résistance*, p. 354: 'ce perpétuel juge d'instruction qu'est l'historien'.)

by the historian as traces related to the past. As in Chinese boxes, the latter experiment includes the former.

In order to analyse this historiographic experiment, I will focus on some trials I am particularly familiar with, conducted by the Roman Inquisition in the sixteenth and seventeenth centuries. These trials are marked by secrecy. Interrogations are secret; proceedings are secret. The defendants do not know the provenance of the accusations raised against them. When, exceptionally, they could rely upon a lawyer who had access to the proceedings, the accusers' names were concealed by initials. Only the judge (the inquisitor, or his vicar) had full control over the trial's development and was able to set up the elements of his 'historiographic experiment'. The other participants (defendants, witnesses) had a very limited knowledge of what was going on in the court: they acted, so to speak, in the dark. Outside the dark was the inquisitor who tested his hypotheses—his biases—in the trial. (Even in this context, initial hypotheses were sometimes disproven.) A few centuries later, these court records are read and analysed by a historian who starts from hypotheses, information and (why not) biases which are widely different from those which can be ascribed to inquisitors, to defendants, to witnesses from the past.

A specific example will hopefully clarify the implications of the analogy between this 'historiographic experiment raised to the square' and double-blind experiments. Many years ago, in the Udine ecclesiastical archives, I came across nearly 50 trials, of different lengths, which took place between the late sixteenth and the late seventeenth centuries. I analysed them in my fist book: *I benandanti* (1966), translated into English as *The Night Battles*. The defendants, men and women, usually peasants, told the inquisitors that they were born with a shirt, that is, wrapped in the caul: therefore, they were 'benandanti' (literally, 'those who go for the good'), compelled to leave 'in spirit' three or four times a year, to fight with fennel branches for the fertility of the crops, against witches and wizards who used sorghum sticks as a weapon. The inquisitors, faced with those unheard-of tales, full of extraordinary details, tried, on the one hand, to convince the benandanti to confess that they were witches and wizards, their alleged enemies; on the other, to admit that the night battles they participated in 'in spirit' were anything but the witches' sabbath. Initially, the benandanti rejected with indignation the inquisitors' oblique suggestions; but later, after a clash which lasted half a century, they ultimately introjected, albeit among strong resistance, the diabolical image which had been imposed on them. The cultural gap between inquisitors and benandanti was filled up, albeit only partially, by violence—in those Friulian trials, mostly symbolical.

The historian (in this case, myself) who tries to interpret those documents knows, at the same time, more or less than the actors involved in the trials: inquisitors, witnesses, benandanti. The inquisitors' intellectual categories look distant, the benandanti's even more. But distance, both intellectual and chronological, is not necessarily an obstacle: it can turn itself into an asset—critical distance. The historian tries to put the past, as the saying goes, in perspective.[26] He will try to avoid as much as possible what E. P. Thompson labelled 'the enormous condescension of posterity'.[27] But the actors on the trials' stage will appear blindly immersed in the limited perspective of their own lives. Seen from the future (and with the dubious benefit of hindsight), the present necessarily looks blind.

What is the aim of the historiographic experiment raised to the square which the historian conducts? Why is he, or she, looking at the evidence? To check a factual reality, comparable to the effectiveness of a drug? Yes and no. The trial's development must be reconstructed in detail, of course, but the historian will especially focus on the background noise: hopes, expectations, fears nourished by benandanti, by witnesses, by judges—and their interaction in the trial. Placebo comes to the forefront. Like in one of those images used by Gestalt psychologists, the relationship between solids and voids, between forefront and background, is subverted: we are confronted with an image which replicates the double-blind experiment in an inverted form.

---

26 Ginzburg, 'Distanza e prospettiva: due metafore' in *Occhiacci di legno*, pp. 171–93.

27 E. P. Thompson, *The Making of the English Working Class* (Harmondsworth: Penguin Books, 1968), p. 13.

6. As I anticipated, the comparison, hypothetical and provisional, between double-blind experiments and historical research did not aim to find analogies: divergences would have been relevant as well. The documents I am talking about are, for many reasons, particularly appropriate to work as tools for a contrastive analysis. They are certainly anomalous, but anomalies can help decipher the norm, since they necessarily include it (not the other way round).

The benandanti trials are based on events which are not only intangible but also, by definition, unattainable to external observers: the lethargies or swoons during which the spirit of those born in a caul left the motionless body to join the nocturnal battles. Those silent experiences, which the benandanti tried to translate into words, came to us through the transcriptions, often inadequate and incomplete, made by the Inquisition's notaries. In some cases, the notaries translated the benandanti's narratives from the Friulian dialect into Italian. Historians, as Bloch pointed out, inevitably rely upon traces, but in this case, this limitation seems particularly acute. The analysis is based on traces which are (a) indirect in a double or triple degree; (b) generated by an event which is by definition untestable, since it is part of an inaccessible private sphere; (c) distorted—one should never forget this—by a context like the Inquisition trial, sometimes dominated by physical pressure (i.e. torture) and always by symbolic violence. Indirect, untestable, distorted data—but, first of all, *data* which are, according to the Latin etymology of the word, *given* rather than constructed as in the double-blind experiment, in which everything is set up from the very beginning, the randomized distribution of drugs and placebos. To sum up: the aims of the historiographic experiment raised to the square and the double-blind experiment are the same: to achieve a certified truth—a scientifically certified truth. But their respective trajectories are different.

Why different? Because the rationality which inspires those who conduct the double-blind experiment aims to put under control other people's emotions: patients', doctors', nurses'. The rationality which inspires the historian aims, on the contrary, to take the actors' emotions as seriously as possible, and then to turn them into an object of analysis. The benandanti trials are literally soaked by those emotions. 'I am all sweaty, I cannot stop sweating because of the great mental effort,' the benandante Michele Soppe told the inquisitor who was trying to make him confess that he had attended the witches' meetings. (After much hesitation, Michele confessed; he died in jail one year after the interrogations, in 1650.)[28]

Clearly, those nocturnal journeys were for the benandanti a deeply intense experience. How can we speak about them—and how

---

28 Carlo Ginzburg, *I benandanti: Ricerche sulla stregoneria e sui culti agrari tra Cinquecento e Seicento* (Turin: Einaudi, 1966), pp. 125–41, in particular, p. 141 [in English: Carlo Ginzburg, *The Night Battles: Witchcraft and Agrarian Cults in the Sixteenth and Seventeenth Centuries* (John and Ann Tedeschi trans) (London: Routledge and Kegan Paul, 1983), p. 131]. See also Dario Visintin, *Michele Soppe benandante* (Santa Maria la Longa (Udine)-Montereale Valcellina (Pordenone): Circolo Culturale Menocchio, 2009).

can we label them? Here, we are confronted with a difficulty which is at the very centre of the historian's craft: the relationship between the historian's idiom and the actors' idiom.[29] Most of the benandanti, men and women, said that they went to their meetings 'in spirit'; but in 1606, Gasparo of Palmanova declared that 'actually it is true that it also seems to me that that I go out as a benandante in a dream.'[30] We are entitled to use a word like 'dreams' (somebody did it): but we have to point out that the benandanti's ecstatic experiences were inscribed in a cultural pattern which left very narrow room for individual variations.[31] Since the word 'dream' means something different for us, it might weaken or suppress the distance between us and them.

These terminological difficulties (a discussion about them could go on and on) have no place whatsoever in the framework of double-blind experiments. As I mentioned before, those experiments often involve animals belonging to species different from

---

29 On this subject, see Carlo Ginzburg, 'Our Words, and Theirs: Reflections on the Historian's Craft, Today', *Cromohs: Cyber Review of Modern Historiography* 18 (March 2014): 97–114.

30 Ginzburg, *I benandanti*, p. 93 (*The Night Battles*, p. 83). Of a more dubious value, since they are linked to a (failed) attempt to escape the inquisitor's accusations, are the words of Menichino della Nota (1591): 'Uno mio barba, detto Olivo della Notta, che è morto, mi disse che io ero nato vestito con una camicia, né mai havendola avuta sono in questo tempo in sogno andato per boschi, per prati, per campi a pascere animali, et su per li spini' (Ginzburg, *I benandanti*, p. 84).

31 Peter Burke, 'Histoire sociale des rêves', *Annales ESC* 28 (1973): 329–42.

ours; they also imply a randomized administration of both the drug to be tested and the placebo. When I received this information from a biologist, I asked why. 'Just in case', he replied. Then he added that a drug may induce in an individual, belonging to any animal species, unforeseeable bodily reactions, which must be controlled by administering a placebo as well.[32] Reflecting on this exchange, I told myself that expectations, fears and hopes are animal reactions which disregard the boundary between nature and culture.

The divergence must be located elsewhere. The human language used by patients or doctors or nurses involved in the double-blind experiment is absolutely irrelevant for the experiment's aims. On the contrary, the language used in the evidence is absolutely crucial to the historian, even in case of silent testimonies: images or objects which must be deciphered through verbal descriptions. The historian relies upon an everyday language which he or she shares with most of the evidence. From a cognitive point of view this contiguity was, according to Bloch, absolutely negative: 'the great advantage of chemistry [over history] is that it deals with realities which, by nature, could not name themselves.'[33] Bloch's irony half-conceals a problem which is not easy to solve. Testimonies from the past confront us with a changing terminology, widely different from the rigid, conventional one usually associated

---

32 See also Harrington, *The Placebo Effect*, pp. 5–6.

33 Bloch, *Apologie pour l'histoirem*: 'C'est que la chimie avait le grand avantage de s'adresser à des réalités incapables, par nature, de se nommer elles-mêmes.'

with natural sciences. Is this terminological fluidity compatible with the rigour of demonstration? Can historical hypotheses be submitted to an objective test, allowing a distinction between truth and falsehood?

7. An answer to those questions will inevitably start from the oft-mentioned analogy between the judge and the historian. Eric Hobsbawm reworked it with strong polemical overtones:

> the procedures of the law court, which insist on the supremacy of the evidence as much as historical researchers, and often in much the same manner, demonstrate that difference between historical fact and falsehood is not ideological [. . .]. When an innocent person is tried for murder, and wishes to prove his or [her] innocence, what is required is the techniques not of the 'postmodern' theorist, but of the old-fashioned historian.[34]

---

34 Eric J. Hobsbawm, 'Identity History is not Enough' in *On History* (New York: New Press, 1997), p. 272 [Eric J. Hobsbawm, *De Historia* (Milan: Rizzoli, 1997), pp. 212–3; the translation is slightly different from the original]. Cited in Dipesh Chakrabarty, *Provincializing Europe: Postcolonial Thought and Historical Difference* (Princeton, NJ: Princeton University Press, 2000), p. 107. The doubts about the notion of proof put forward in Chakrabarty, *Provincializing Europe*, pp. 102–06, have been met with criticisms (which I fully share) by Natalie Zemon Davis, *La passione della storia: Un dialogo con Denis Crouzet* (Angiolina Arru and Sofia Boesch Gajano eds) (Rome: Viella, 2007), pp. 82–3. For a toned-down response, see Dipesh Chakrabarty, 'The Politics and Possibility of Historical Knowledge: Continuing the Conversation', *Postcolonial Studies* 14 (2011): 243–50; in particular, pp. 247–8.

According to Dipesh Chakrabarty, who quoted this passage, Hobsbawm 'provides some unwitting evidence of history's close ties to law and other instruments of government'. A bizarre remark, for two reasons. To assume that Hobsbawm is unaware of the ties, ancient and well known, between history and law, is gratuitous; equally gratuitous is Chakrabarty's suggestion, which immediately follows, that such ties would imply that, in order to write the 'history of minorities', one should get rid of traditional methods of proof.[35] (According to this kind of logic, the very idea of writing a 'history of minorities' should be discarded, since, for some millennia, writing has been closely connected to the instruments of government.) Walter Benjamin's line, often quoted as a mantra—'Rub history against the grain'—means, first of all, to read historical testimonies not only but *also* against the intentions of those who produced them.[36] The historiographical experiment raised to the square I mentioned before, which analyses Inquisition trials trying to rescue the voices of persecuted minorities, may be placed in this perspective. Some elements which the inquisitors (those distant experimentors) were unable to control, may open up, today, the possibility of a reading which will be different from theirs.

---

35 'This is why Hobsbawm would argue that minority histories must also conform to the protocols of "good history",' wrote Chakrabarty. See *Provincializing Europe*, p. 107. Chakrabarty does not realize that Hobsbawm uses the expression 'good history' in an ironic sense.

36 Carlo Ginzburg, *Il filo e le tracce: Vero falso finto* (Milan: Feltrinelli, 2006), pp. 9–10.

8. I have been tempted, for a moment, as a homage to Arnaldo Momigliano's famous essay 'History between Medicine and Rhetoric', to place these reflections under a title such as 'History between Medicine and Law'; but I would not like to seem presumptuous. What for a long time fascinated me in double-blind experiments has been the coexistence of a concern for proof (shared with historians and judges) and an acute, and much more unusual, awareness of the possibility that those who do research may unwillingly distort its results through a projection of expectations and biases, along with hypotheses and schemata. One must sterilize the instruments of analysis, I have been repeating for many years; but the first instrument which must be sterilized is, of course, the researcher himself (or herself). This difficult process of self-control is symbolically embodied in the split between those who conduct in full awareness the double-blind experiment, and those who perform it (doctors, nurses and so forth) in full ignorance. I will come back in a moment to this asymmetry and its implications. Here, I would like to stress once again that the positive outcome of the experiment depends on the darkness in which it takes place—therefore from the impossibility of distinguishing between medicament and placebo. Otherwise, the data will be contaminated and the experiment will fail.

The nightmare of data contamination will ring a bell for those who are even vaguely familiar with the discipline dealing with the transmission of texts. 'No specific has yet been discovered against contamination,' reads the often quoted, closing sentence of the second edition (1949) of Paul Maas *Textkritik* (Textual Criticism), a slim book which displayed, with concise, geometric elegance, the eminently technical features of textual philology.[37] But the implications of this seemingly arcane discipline intersect at every moment of our daily lives. We endlessly deal with duplicated texts which recapitulate in various forms the stages of a long historical trajectory: from handwritten transcription to print to electronic cut-and-paste. A series of metaphorical exchanges between biology and textual criticism, and the other way round—'families' or 'genealogical trees' of manuscripts, 'copy ' or 'duplication' of DNA—reveal a deep theme of the culture we belong.[38]

The ideal model of textual transmission analysed by Paul Maas implies, on the one hand, that no copyist contaminated, that is, compared different manuscripts; on the other, that all copyists made mistakes.[39] A copyist's right conjecture (not pointed out as such) may look like a contamination: therefore, it would disturb the mechanical reconstruction, which is Maas' aim, of the *stemma codicum* or family tree which describes the relationship between

---

37 Paul Maas, *Critica del testo* (Nello Martinelli trans.; Giorgio Pasquali pref.) ('A Retrospective Look 1956' and a note by L. Canfora) (Firenze: La Monnier, 1990). The quoted sentence is on p. 62; see the comment by Pasquali, pp. 8–9, which recalls the literal translation: 'no grass has yet grown against contamination'. Maas' work continues to be an essential point of reference: see Roberto Angelini, 'Fenomenologia della copia', *Studi medievalis* 3(51) (2010): 329–47.

38 See Carlo Ginzburg, 'Family Resemblances and Family Trees: Two Cognitive Metaphors', *Critical Inquiry* 30 (Spring 2004): 537–56. I am working on a book on this theme.

39 Maas, *Critica del testo*, p. 4, paragraph 6.

different manuscripts or groups of manuscripts.[40] In other words, according to Maas' model the philologist must try to emendate, on the basis of conjectures (obviously not gratuitous but based on the knowledge of the author's style or *usus scribendi*) corrupted textual passages; copyists must limit themselves to copying.[41] Their inevitable mistakes, which Maas classified according to labels that have become part of standard philological lexicon, pave the way to a reconstruction of the manuscript's families, a preliminary step to a conjectural reconstruction of the archetype.

9. A textual philologist who works on the mistakes of copyists whose activity as potential philologists is regarded a disturbance: the model which emerges from Maas' crystal-clear prose will inevitably evoke the double-blind experiment—in this case, aimed to the reconstruction of the past. A completely different perspective was put forward by Giorgio Pasquali, first in his review of Maas' *Textkritik* (double the length of the volume reviewed), then in his great book *Storia della tradizione e critica del testo* (History of Textual Tradition and Textual Criticism, 1934, 1952). The second edition included an essay by Maas, enlarged by the author and translated by Pasquali himself: a detail witnessing the mutual respect between the two scholars. The strong divergence of their approach was immediately evident. Pasquali emphasized his distance from Maas in the very first page of his book: 'In order to turn a set of logical,

40 Maas, *Critica del testo*, p. 12, paragraph 12.

41 Maas, *Critica del testo*, pp. 21–3, paragraph 18.

therefore abstract norms into a historically based method, one must not refrain from details.' On the basis of a great number of closely analysed cases, Pasquali showed that contamination, that is, comparison between different manuscripts, which Maas had excluded from his assumptions, was common practice since antiquity. Copyists (better to say, ancient editors) compared, made conjectures, interpreted difficult passages. Hence Pasquali's conclusion: a close inquiry of manuscript testimonies—in other words, the history of the manuscript tradition—is the necessary preliminary of textual criticism. The close connection between those two stages emerged from Pasquali's book, announced in its very title.[42]

This brief and absolutely inadequate presentation of the divergence between Pasquali and Maas is apparently unrelated to the topic of my reflections—but only apparently. In fact, that divergence points to the example I started from: Gombrich's comparison between the nineteenth-century lithograph representing the western facade of the Chartres Cathedral and the photograph of the same facade. As you may recall, starting from the undeliberate distortion of the copyist-lithographer—the Romanesque windows turned into Gothic ones—I extended to all testimonies the implications of Gombrich's example: to evaluate the referential value of a testimony we must first analyse what the testimony says, above all undeliberately,

42 Arsenio Frugoni, who had participated in Pasquali's Pisan seminars, transmitted a vivid echo of his teaching (as I understand only now) by reinterpreting it in an original way.

about itself. As you may see, my argument was a paraphrasis and a generalization of Pasquali's—the history of tradition is the necessary premise of textual criticism.

Pasquali's book has never been translated, although it widely circulated among classical philologists of all countries. What has been translated, fortunately, is *The Genesis of Lachmann's Method* by Sebastiano Timpanaro, a highly original scholar who had been Pasquali's pupil, and developed and updated his book.[43] In Timpanaro's harsh and sometimes unjustified criticism addressed to Maas' *Textkritik*, I am inclined to see, besides a thoughtful defence of Pasquali's perspective, a political subtext.[44] Timpanaro, a leftwing militant, could have no sympathy for a model which denied the copyists' intellectual autonomy, ascribing it exclusively to the philologist—therefore isolating textual philology from the tradition which had made it possible.

---

43 Sebastiano Timpanaro, *La genesi del metodo del Lachmann* (Elio Montanari intro.) (Firenze: Le Monnier 2003[1963]). And see G. W. Most's important introduction to the American edition he translated and edited: Glenn W. Most, Editor's Introduction to Sebastiano Timpanaro, *The Genesis of Lachmann's Method* (Glenn W. Most trans., ed. and intro.) (Chicago: University of Chicago Press, 2005), pp. 1–33. I have not seen the German translation: Sebastiano Timpanaro, *Die Entstehung der Lachmannschen Methode* (Dieter Irmer trans.) (Hamburg: Buske Verlag, 1971).

44 See Timpanaro, *La genesi*, p. 164 (addendum a) (about Maas). See the beautiful book by Timpanaro on these themes: Sebastiano Timpanaro, *Il lapsus freudiano: Psicoanalisi e filologia testuale* (Firenze: La Nuova Italia, 1975). On the double blind as a political metaphor, I refer to an exchange in Carlo Ginzburg and Vittorio Foa, *Un dialogo* (Milan: Feltrinelli, 2003), pp. 130–2.

10. Double-blind experiments have been criticized from an ethical point of view. As has been argued, they violate the covenant of trust on which the relationship between doctor and patient is based. But the attempt to control or suppress specific data for a cognitive purpose is, if I am not mistaken, part of the very idea of a scientific experiment: an idea which must be defended against the fashionable, often superficial scepticism which has, for decades, affected (or infected) the humanities and social sciences. The cognitive and political asymmetry implied in the experiment is probably inevitable. Much more open to criticism is, if I am not mistaken, the scientific status which those who conduct the double-blind experiment tacitly, and irrevocably, ascribe to themselves.

Today, few would believe that history is the teacher of life. But history contiues to teach us a sense of limits. Any individual—be it a poet, a scholar, a politician—moves within a horizon which inevitably includes an uncontrolled spot, a blind spot.[45] The model based on the double-blind experiment does not take this blind spot into account. But experience teaches us that an experiment—any experiment—can be always re-opened, starting from different questions. Research is endless.

45 I investigated a test case in Carlo Ginzburg, 'Dante's Blind Spot (*Inferno* XVI–XVII)' in Sara Fortuna et al. (eds), *Dante's Pluringualism: Authority, Knowledge, Subjectivity* (London: Routledge, 2010), pp. 149–63.

Bibliography

Civilization and Barbarism

AQUINAS, Thomas. *Commentaria in libros octo Politicorum Aristotelis*. Rome, 1492[c.1272].

——. *In libros Politicorum Aristotelis expositio* (Raimondo Spiazzi ed.). Turin: Marietti, 1951[c.1272].

ARISTOTLE. *Politics* (H. Rackham trans.). Cambridge: Harvard University Press, 1959[c.325 BCE].

——. *De interpretatione* (Boethius trans.). Berlin: De Gruyter, 2014.

BACCELLI, Luca. 'Guerra e diritti: Vitoria, Las Casas e la conquista dell'America'. *Quaderni fiorentini per la storia del pensiero giuridico moderno* 37 (2008): 67–101.

BENVENISTE, Émile. *Noms d'agent et noms d'action en indo-européen*. Paris: Adrien-Maisonneuve, 1948.

——. *Le vocabulaire des institutions indo-européennes*, VOL. 1. Paris: Minuit, 1969.

GINZBURG, Carlo. *Wooden Eyes: Nine Reflections on Distance*. New York: Columbia University Press, 2001.

——. 'Lost in Translation: Us and Them'. *Hermitage* 2 (2006): 20–2.

——. 'Le forbici di Warburg' in Maria Luisa Catoni, Carlo Ginzburg, Luca Giuliani and Salvatore Settis, *Tre figure: Achille, Meleagro, Cristo*. Milan: Feltrinelli, 2013, pp. 109–32.

——. 'Intricate Readings: Machiavelli, Aristotle, Thomas Aquinas'. *Journal of the Warburg and Courtauld Institutes* 78 (2015): 157–72.

——. 'Casuistry, For and Against: Pascal's *Provinciales* and Their Aftermath'. Tanner Lectures, 2014–15.

HERODOTUS. *Herodotus*, VOL. 2 (Alfred Denis Godley trans.). Cambridge, MA: Harvard University Press, 1982[c. 425 BCE].

HUMPHREYS, Sally. 'Law, Custom and Culture in Herodotus'. *Arethusa* 20 (1987): 211–20.

LAROCHE, Emmanuel. *Histoire de la racine 'Nem' en grec ancien: nemo, nemesis, nomos, nomizo*. Paris: Klincksieck, 1949.

LAS CASAS, Bartolomé de. *Apologia* in Juan Ginés de Sepúlveda and Bartolomé de Las Casas, *Apologia* (Angel Losada ed. and trans.). Madrid: Editora Nacional, 1975[1551].

——. *Obras completes, Volume 10: Tratados de 1552* (Ramón Hernández and Lorenzo Galmés eds). Madrid: Alianza, 1992[1552].

LLOYD, Geoffrey Ernest Richard. *Polarity and Analogy: Two Types of Argumentation in Early Greek Thought*. Cambridge: Cambridge University Press, 1966.

MACHIAVELLI, Niccolò. *The Prince* (Harvey C. Mansfield trans.). Chicago: University of Chicago Press, 1998[1513].

MARTIN, Conor. 'The Vulgate Text of Aquinas's Commentary on Aristotle's *Politics*'. *Dominican Studies* 5 (1952): 35–64.

MOMIGLIANO, Arnaldo. 'The Fault of the Greeks' in *Sesto contributo alla storia degli studi classici e del mondo antico, Vol. 2*. Rome: Ed. di Storia e Letteratura, 1980, pp. 509–24.

The New Jerusalem Bible (Henry Wansbrough ed.). New York: Doubleday, 1985.

NIPPEL, Wilfried. 'La costruzione dell' "altro"' in Salvatore Settis (ed.), *I Greci: Storia, cultura, arte, società, Volume 1: Noi e i Greci*. Turin: Einaudi, 1996, pp. 165–96.

PAGDEN, Anthony. *The Fall of Natural Man: The American Indian and the Origins of Comparative Ethnology*. Cambridge: Cambridge University Press, 1986.

PLATO. *The Statesman* (Harold N. Fowler trans.). Cambridge, MA: Harvard University Press, 1975[c.350 BCE].

ROBINSON, Thomas M. *Contrasting Arguments: An Edition of the* Dissoi Logoi. New York: Arno Press, 1979.

SEPÚLVEDA, Juan Ginés de. *Apologia Joannis Genesii Sepulvedae pro libro de iustis belli causis* in Juan Ginés de Sepúlveda and Bartolomé de Las Casas, *Apologia* (Angel Losada ed. and trans.). Madrid: Editora Nacional, 1975[1550].

——. *Democrate secondo ovvero sulle giuste cause di guerra* (Domenico Taranto ed.). Macerata: Quodlibet, 2009[1544].

TODOROV, Tzvetan. *La Conquête de l'Amérique*. Paris: Seuil, 1982.

TUCK, Richard. *The Rights of War and Peace: Political Thought and the International Order from Grotius to Kant*. Oxford: Oxford University Press, 1999.

UNTERSTEINER, Mario. *I sofisti: testimonianze e frammenti*, VOL. 2. Milan: Mondadori, 1967.

VASOLI, Cesare. 'Leonardo Bruni' in *Dizionario biografico degli italiani*, VOL. 14. Rome: Istituto della Enciclopedia Italiana, 1972, pp. 618–33.

The Soul of Brutes: A Sixteenth-Century Debate

ALIGHIERI, Dante. *La Commedia, Volume 2: Inferno* (Giorgio Petrocchi ed.). Milan: Mondadori, 1966–67.

ANNAS, Julia. *Hellenistic Philosophy of Mind*. Berkeley: University of California Press, 1992.

AQUINAS, Thomas. *Sancti Thomae Aquinatis in Aristotelis librum de Anima commentarium* (Angelo M. Pirotta ed.). Casale: Marietti, 1979.

ARISTOTLE. *De republica libri VIII* (Juan Ginés de Sepúlveda ed.) (for Philip, Prince of Spain). Paris, 1548.

——. *Art of Rhetoric* (J. H. Freese trans.). Cambridge, MA: Harvard University Press, 1926 (Loeb Classical Library 193).

——. *On the Soul. Parva Naturalia. On Breath* (W. S. Hett trans.). Cambridge, MA: Harvard University Press, 1957 (Loeb Classical Library 288).

——. *Politics* (H. Rackham trans.). Cambridge, MA: Harvard University Press, 1959.

——. *L'anima* (Giancarlo Movia ed.). Naples: Luigi Loffredo, 1979.

BAYLE, Pierre. *Dictionnaire historique et critique*. Basel: Chez Jean Louis Brandmuller, 1741.

BENVENISTE, Émile. *Il vacabolario delle istituzioni indoeuropee, I* (M. Liborio ed. and trans.). Turin: Einaudi, 1976.

CAMASSA, Giorgio. '*Phantasia* da Platone ai Neoplatonici' in Marta Fattori and Massimo Bianchi (eds), *Phantasia-Imaginatio*. Rome: Edizioni dell'Ateneo, 1988, pp. 24–55.

CAVAZZA, Silvano. 'Girolamo Rorario e il dialogo "Julius exclusus"'. *Memorie storiche forogiuliesi* 60 (1980): 129–64;

EMPIRICUS, Sextus. *Outlines of Scepticism* (Julia Annas and Jonathan Barnes eds and trans). Cambridge: Cambridge University Press, 1994.

ERASMUS, Desiderius. *Apophthegmata* in *Opera* (Jean Le Clerc ed.). Lugduni Batavorum Vander, 1706.

——. 'Socratis gallus aut callus' in *Adagia* in *Opera* (Jean Le Clerc ed.). Lugduni Batavorum Vander, 1706.

FREDE, Dorothea. 'The Cognitive Role of *Phantasia* in Aristotle' in Martha C. Nussbaum and Amelie Oksenberg Rorty (eds), *Essays on Aristotle's De Anima*. Oxford: Clarendon Press, 1992, pp. 279–95.

GARIN, Eugenio. *Storia della filosofia italiana*, VOL. 2. Turin: Einaudi, 1966.

——. *Dal Rinascimento all'Illuminismo*. Pisa: Nistri-Lischi, 1970.

GELLI, Giambattista. *La Circe* in *Dialoghi* (Roberto Tissoni ed.). Bari: Laterza, 1967.

GINZBURG, Carlo. 'Montaigne, Cannibals and Grottoes'. *History and Anthropology* 6(2–3) (1993): 125–55.

——. *Wooden Eyes: Nine Reflections on Distance*. New York: Columbia University Press, 2001.

——. 'The High and the Low' in *Clues, Myths, and the Historical Method* (John Tedeschi and Anne Tedeschi trans). Baltimore, MD: Johns Hopkins University Press, 2013, pp. 54–69.

GLIOZZI, Giuliano. *Adamo e il nuovo mondo*. Firenze: La Nuova Italia, 1977.

KRISTELLER, Paul Oskar. 'Between the Italian Renaissance and the French Enlightenment: Gabriel Naudé as an Editor'. *Renaissance Quarterly* 32(1) (Spring 1979): 41–72.

LABARRIÈRE, Jean-Louise. 'Imagination humaine et imagination animale chez Aristotle'. *Phronesis* 29(1) (1984): 17–49.

——. 'Raison humaine et intelligence animale dans la philosophie grecque'. *Terrain* 34 (March 2000) (*Les animaux pensent-ils?*): 107–22.

LAERTIUS, Diogenes. *El libro della vita de philosophi et delle loro elegantissime sententie extracto da D. Lahertio et da altri antiquissimi auctori*. Florence: Franciscum de Bonaccursiis et Antonium Venetum, 1488.

——. *Lives of the Eminent Philosophers*, VOL. 2 (Robert D. Hicks trans.). Cambridge, MA: Harvard University Press, 1979.

LLOYD, G. E. R. *Polarity and Analogy: Two Types of Argumentation in Early Greek Thought*. Cambridge: Cambridge University Press, 1971.

MACHIAVELLI, Niccolo. *Opere letterarie* (Luigi Blasucci ed.). Milan: Adelphi, 1964.

MODRAK, Deborah. 'Φαντασία Reconsidered', *Archiv für die Geschichte der Philosophie* 68(1) (1986): 47–69.

MONTAIGNE, Michel de. *Essais* (Albert Thibaudet ed.). Paris: Gallimard, 1950.

——. *The Complete Essays* (M. A. Screech trans.). London: Penguin Books, 1991.

NARDI, Bruno. 'I corsi manoscritti di lezioni e il ritratto di Pietro Pomponazzi' in *Studi su Pietro Pomponazzi*. Firenze: Felice Le Monnier, 1965, pp. 3–53.

NUSSBAUM, Martha C. 'The Role of *Phantasia* in Aristotle's Explanations of Action' in *Aristotle's* De Motu Animalium (Martha C. Nussbaum ed.). Princeton, NJ: Princeton University Press, 1978, pp. 221–69.

PASCHINI, Pio. 'Un pordenonese nunzio papale nel secolo XVI: Gerolamo Rorario'. *Memorie storiche forogiuliesi* 30 (1934): 169–216.

PARENTE, Margherita Isnardi. 'Le obiezioni di Stratone al "Fedone" e l'epistemologia peripatetica nel primo ellenismo'. *Rivista di filologia e istruzione classica* 105 (1977): 287–306.

PIGLER, Andor. 'The Importance of Iconographical Exactitude'. *The Art Bulletin* 21 (1939): 228–37.

——. *Barockthemen: eine Auswahl von Verzeichnissen zur Ikonographie des 17. und 18. Jahrhunderts*. Budapest: Akademiai Kiado, 1974.

PINOTTI, Patrizia. 'Gli animali in Platone' in Silvana Castignone and Giuliana Lanata (eds), *Filosofia e animali nel mondo antico*. Pisa: ETS, 1994.

PLUTARCH. *Plutarchi Chironei Dialogus* (Dominicus Bonominus trans.). Brescia: Angelum Britannicum, 27 May 1503. (BUB: Aula V. Tab I . F. I. VOL. 423.2, bound with ISOCRATES, *De regno gubernando* (Dominicus Bonominus trans.). Brescia: Angelum Britannicum, 27 May 1503.

——. *Regum et imperatorum Aphtegmata Raphaele Regio interprete; Plutarchi Laconica Apophtegmata Raphaele Regio interprete; Plutarchi Dialogus in quo animalia bruta ratione uti monstrantur, Joanne Regio interprete;*

Raphaelis Regii apologia, in qua quattuor hae questiones potissimum edisseruntur... Venice: Georgio Rusconi, 11 October 1508. Vatican: Incun. IV. 573 (3).

——. *Dialogo di Plutarco circa l'avertire de gl'animali quali sieno più accorti, o li terrestri, o li marini, di greco in latino et di latino in volgare, nuovamente tradotto, et con ogni diligentia stampato.* Venice: 1545.

——. *Moralia*, VOL. 12 (Harold F. Cherniss and William C. Helmbold trans). Cambridge, MA: Harvard University Press, 1957.

POPHAM, A. E. *Catalogue of the Drawings of Parmigianino*, VOL. 1. New Haven, CT, and London: Yale University Press, 1973.

PROSPERI, Adriano. *Tra evangelismo e controriforma: Gian Matteo Giberti (1495–1543).* Rome: Edizioni di storia e letteratura, 2011.

REPICI, Luciana. *La natura e l'anima: Saggi su Stratone di Lampsaco.* Turin: Tirrenia Stampatori, 1988.

RORARIUS, Hieronymus. *Quod animalia bruta ratione utuntur melius homine*, 2 VOLS (Gabriel Naudé ed.). Paris: Sébastien Cramoisy, 1648.

SCHIANCHI, Lucia Fornari and Sylvia Ferino Pagden (eds). *Parmigianino e il manierismo europeo.* Milan: Silvana, 2004.

SCHOFIELD, Malcolm. 'Aristotle on the Imagination' in Martha C. Nussbaum and Amelie Oksenberg Rorty (eds), *Essays on Aristotle's De Anima.* Oxford: Clarendon Press, 1992, pp. 249–77.

SEPÚLVEDA, Juan Ginés de. *Democrates secundus sive de justis belli causis* (Angel Losada ed. and trans.). Madrid: Instituto Francisco de Vitoria, 1951.

SHAKESPEARE, William. *Hamlet* (Ann Thompson and Neil Taylor eds). London: Arden Shakespeare, 2020.

SORABJI, Richard. *Animal Minds and Human Morals: The Origins of the Western Debate.* Ithaca, NY: Cornell University Press, 1993.

STRATO of Lampsacus. *Die Schule des Aristoteles, Texte und Kommentar* [series], *Volume 5: Straton von Lampsakos* (Fritz Wehrli ed.). Basel: Schwabe, 1950.

VASARI, Giorgio. *Le opere di Giorgio Vasari*, VOL. 5 (Gaetano Milanesi ed.). Firenze: Sansoni, 1976[1906].

WATSON, Gerald. 'Φαντασία in Aristotle, De Anima 3.3'. *The Classical Quarterly* 32(1) (1982): 100–13.

WIND, Edgar. 'Homo Platonis'. *Journal of the Warburg* 1(3) (1937–38): 261.

Calvino, Manzoni and the Gray Zone

BELPOLITI, Marco. *Primo Levi*. Milan: Mondadori, 1998.

BUCCIANTINI, Massimo. *Esperimento Auschwitz: Auschwitz Experiment*. Turin: Einaudi, 2011.

CALVINO, Italo. Review. *La Repubblica*, 11 July 1981.

——. 'Piccola Guida alla Piccola Cosmogonia' [Afterword] in Raymond Queneau, *Piccola cosmogonia portatile* (Sergio Solmi trans.). Turin: Einaudi, 1982.

——. *I libri degli altri* (Giovanni Tesio ed.). Turin: Einaudi, 1991.

——. *Romanzi e racconti*, VOL. 1 (Mario Barenghi and Bruno Falcetto eds). Milan: Arnoldo Mondadori Editore, 1991.

——. Afterword to Primo Levi, *The Search for Roots: A Personal Anthology*. Chicago: Ivan R Dee, 2001.

——. *Italo Calvino: Letters, 1941–1985* (Martin McLaughlin trans.). Princeton, NJ: Princeton University Press, 2013.

CASES, Cesare. 'L'ordine delle cose e l'ordine delle parole' in Ernesto Ferrero (ed.), *Primo Levi: un'antologia della critica*. Turin: Einaudi, 1997.

FERRERO, Ernesto. *Rhêmes o della felicità*. Turin: Liaison, 2008.

LANGBEIN, Hermann. *People in Auschwitz* (Harry Zohn trans.). Chapel Hill: University of North Carolina Press, 2004.

LEVI, Primo. *Opere*, 2 VOLS (Marco Belpoliti ed.). Turin: Einaudi, 1977, 1997.

——. *L'altrui mestiere*. Turin: Einaudi, 1985.

——. 'Capire non è perdonare'. *La Stampa*, 26 July 1986.

——. *The Drowned and the Saved* (Raymond Rosenthal trans.). New York: Vintage, 1989.

——. *Other People's Trades* (Raymond Rosenthal trans.). London: Abacus, 1991.

——. 'Ex-Chemist' in *Other People's Trades* (Raymond Rosenthal trans.). London: Abacus, 1991.

——. 'Ritual and Laughter' in *Other People's Trades* (Raymond Rosenthal trans.). London: Abacus, 1991, pp. 196–200.

——. 'Calvino, Queneau e le scienze' in *Opere*, VOL. 2 (Marco Belpoliti ed.). Turin: Einaudi, 1997, pp. 1344–6.

——. *Conversazioni e interviste: 1963–1987* (Marco Belpoliti ed.). Turin: Einaudi, 1997.

——. *The Periodic Table* (Raymond Rosenthal trans.). New York: Penguin Books, 2000.

——. *The Voice of Memory: Interviews, 1961–1987* (Marco Belpoliti and David Gordon eds). New York: Polity, 2000.

——. 'A Conversation with Primo Levi (1979)', interview by Giuseppe Grassano, in *The Voice of Memory: Interviews, 1961–1987* (Marco Belpoliti and David Gordon eds). New York: Polity, 2000, pp. 121–35.

——. '*The Drowned and the Saved* (1986)', interview by Giorgio Calcagno, in *The Voice of Memory: Interviews, 1961–1987* (Marco Belpoliti and David Gordon eds). New York: Polity, 2000, pp. 109–13.

——. *The Search for Roots: A Personal* Anthology. Chicago: Ivan R. Dee, 2001.

——. *'If This Is a Man' and 'The Truce'* (Stuart Woolf trans.). London: Abacus, 2002.

——. *The Black Hole of Auschwitz* (Sharon Wood trans.). Malden, MA: Polity, 2005.

——. 'Arbeit Macht Frei (1959)' in *The Black Hole of Auschwitz* (Sharon Wood trans.). Malden, MA: Polity, 2005.

——. 'Preface to Presser's *The Night of the Girondins*' in *The Black Hole of Auschwitz* (Sharon Wood trans.). Malden, MA: Polity, 2005.

——. 'Preface to H. Langbein's *People in Auschwitz*' in *The Black Hole of Auschwitz* (Sharon Wood trans.). Malden, MA: Polity, 2005.

——. *La zone grise: entretien avec Anna Bravo et Federico Cereja*. Paris: Payot and Rivages, 2014.

MANZONI, Alessandro. *A Vindication of Catholic Morality*. London: Keating and Brown, 1836.

MENGALDO, Pier Vicenzo. 'Lingua e scrittura in Levi' in Per Primo Levi. Turin: Einaudi, 2019, pp. 233–42.

MESNARD, Philippe. *Primo Levi: Le passage d'un témoin*. Paris: Fayard, 2011.

POLI, Gabriella and Giorgio Calcagno. *Echi di una voce perduta*. Milan: Mursia, 1992.

QUENEAU, Raymond. *Petite cosmogonie portative*. Paris: Gallimard, 1950.

——. *Piccola cosmogonia portatile* (Sergio Solmi trans.). Turin: Einaudi, 1982.

RUFFINI, Francesco. *La vita religiosa di Alessandro Manzoni*, 2 VOLS. Bari: G. Laterza, 1931.

SISMONDI, Jean Charles Léonard de. *Histoire des républiques italiennes du Moyen Age*, VOL. 16. Paris: Treuttel et Wurtz, 1818.

SODI, Risa. 'An Interview with Primo Levi'. *Partisan Review* 54(3) (1987).

Schema and Bias: A Historian's Reflection on Double-Blind Experiments

ANGELINI, Roberto. 'Fenomenologia della copia'. *Studi medievali* 3(51) (2010): 329–47.

BANN, Stephen. *Parallel Lines: Printmakers, Painters and Photographers in Nineteenth-Century France*. New Haven, NC, and London: Yale University Press, 2001.

BENEDETTI, Fabrizio, Helen S. Mayberg, Tor D. Wager, Christian S. Stohler and Jon-Kar Zubieta. 'Neurobiological Mechanisms of the Placebo Effect'. *The Journal of Neuroscience* (9 November 2005): 10390–402.

BLOCH, Marc. *Apologia della storia o mestiere di storico*. Turin: Einaudi, 1950.

——. 'Pour une histoire comparée des sociétés européennes' in *Mélanges historiques* (Charles-Edmond Perrin ed.). Paris: Service d' Edition et de Vente des Publications de l'Education, 1963, pp. 16–40.

——. *Apologie pour l'histoire ou Métier d'historien* in *L'Histoire, la Guerre, la Résistance*. Paris: Gallimard, 1986.

BURKE, Peter. 'Histoire sociale des rêves'. *Annales ESC* 28 (1973): 329–42.

CANFORA, Luciano. *Togliatti e i dilemmi della politica*. Bari: Laterza, 1989.

CATONI, M. L. *La comunicazione non verbale nella Grecia antica*. Turin: Bollati Boringhieri, 2008[2005].

CHAKRABARTY, Dipesh. *Provincializing Europe: Postcolonial Thought and Historical Difference*. Princeton, NJ: Princeton University Press, 2000.

——. 'The Politics and Possibility of Historical Knowledge: Continuing the Conversation'. *Postcolonial Studies* 14 (2011): 243–50.

DAVIS, Natalie Zemon. *La passione della storia: Un dialogo con Denis Crouzet* (Angiolina Arru and Sofia Boesch Gajano eds). Rome: Viella, 2007.

DIAMOND, Jared, and James A. Robinson (eds). *Natural Experiments of History*. Cambridge, MA: Belknap Press of Harvard University Press, 2010.

FERRAJOLI, Luigi. *Diritto e ragione: Teoria del garantismo penale*. Bari: Laterza, 1989.

GINZBURG, Carlo. *I benandanti: Ricerche sulla stregoneria e sui culti agrari tra Cinquecento e Seicento*. Turin: Einaudi, 1966.

——. *The Night Battles: Witchcraft and Agrarian Cults in the Sixteenth and Seventeenth Centuries* (John and Ann Tedeschi trans). London: Routledge and Kegan Paul, 1983.

——. 'Spie: Radici di un paradigma indiziario' [1979] in *Miti, emblemi, spie: morfologia e storia*. Turin: Einaudi, 1984, pp. 158–209.

——. *Il giudice e lo storico*. Turin: Einaudi, 1991.

——. *Occhiacci di legno: Nove riflessioni sulla distanza*. Milan: Feltrinelli, 1998.

——. 'Distanza e prospettiva: due metafore' in *Occhiacci di legno: Nove riflessioni sulla distanza*. Milan: Feltrinelli, 1998, pp. 171–93.

——. 'Family Resemblances and Family Trees: Two Cognitive Metaphors'. *Critical Inquiry* 30 (Spring 2004): 537–56.

——. *Il filo e le tracce: Vero falso finto*. Milan: Feltrinelli, 2006.

——. *Paura reverenza terrore. Rileggere Hobbes oggi*. Parma: Monte Universita Parma, 2008.

——. 'Dante's Blind Spot (*Inferno XVI-XVII*)' in Sara Fortuna, Manuele Gragnolati and Jurgen Trabant (eds), *Dante's Pluringualism: Authority, Knowledge, Subjectivity*. London: Routledge, 2010, pp. 149–63.

——. 'Our Words, and Theirs: Reflections on the Historian's Craft, Today'. *Cromohs - Cyber Review of Modern Historiography* 18 (March 2014): 97–114.

——, and Vittorio Foa. *Un dialogo*. Milan: Feltrinelli, 2003.

GOMBRICH, E. H. *Art and Illusion: A Study in the Psychology of Pictorial Representation*. London: Phaidon Press, 1962[1960].

——. 'Standards of Truth: The Arrested Image and the Moving Eye' in W. J. T. Mitchell (ed.), *The Language of Images*. Chicago: University of Chicago Press, 1980, pp. 181–217

——. 'Image and Code: Limits of Conventionalism in Pictorial Representation' in *The Image and the Eye: Further Studies in the Psychology of Pictorial Representation*. Oxford: Phaidon Press, 1982, pp. 278–97.

——. 'Experiment and Experience in the Arts' in *The Image and the Eye: Further Studies in the Psychology of Pictorial Representation*. Oxford: Phaidon Press, 1982, pp. 215–43.

——. *L'immagine e l'occhio*. Turin: Einaudi, 1985.

HAHN, R. A. 'The Nocebo Phenomenon: Scope and Foundations' in Anne Harrington (ed.), *The Placebo Effect: An Interdisciplinary Exploration*. Cambridge, MA: Harvard University Press, 2000[1997], pp. 56–76.

HARRINGTON, Anne (ed.). *The Placebo Effect: An Interdisciplinary Exploration*. Cambridge, MA: Harvard University Press, 2000[1997].

HOBSBAWM, Eric J. 'Identity History is not Enough' in *On History*. New York: New Press, 1997.

——. *De Historia*. Milan: Rizzoli, 1997.

KAPTCHUK, T. J. 'Intentional Ignorance: A History of Blind Assessment and Placebo Controls in Medicine'. *Bulletin of the History of Medicine* 72 (1988): 389–433.

KLINGENDER, Francis D. *Goya in the Democratic Tradition*. New York: Sidgwick & Jackson, 1968[1948].

MAAS, Paul. *Critica del testo* (Nello Martinelli trans., Giorgio Pasquali pref.). Firenze: La Monnier, 1990.

MITCHELL, W. J. T. *Iconology: Image, Text, Ideology*. Chicago: University of Chicago Press, 1986.

MOMIGLIANO, Arnaldo. 'History between Medicine and Rhetoric' [1985] in *Ottavo contributo alla storia degli studi clasiici e del mondo antico*. Rome: Edizioni di storia e letteratura, 1987, pp. 13–25.

MOST, Glenn W. Introduction to Sebastiano Timpanaro, *The Genesis of Lachmann's Method* (Glenn W. Most ed., trans. and introd.). Chicago: University of Chicago Press, 2005, pp. 1–33.

ROBINSON, James A., Daron Acemoglu, Simon Johnson and Davide Cantoni. 'From Ancien Régime to Capitalism: The French Revolution as a Natural Experiment' in Jared Diamond and James A. Robinson (eds), *Natural Experiments of History*. Cambridge, MA: The Belknap Press of Harvard University Press, 2010, pp. 221–56.

SHAPIRO, Arthur K. 'A Contribution to a History of the Placebo Effect'. *Behavioral Science* 5 (1960): 109–35.

——, and Elaine Shapiro. *The Powerful Placebo: From Ancient Priest to Modern Physician*. Baltimore, MD: Johns Hopkins University Press, 1997.

——, and Elaine Shapiro. 'The Placebo: Is It Much Ado About Nothing?' in Anne Harrington (ed.), *The Placebo Effect: An Interdisciplinary Exploration*. Cambridge, MA: Harvard University Press, 2000[1997], pp. 12–36.

SOLLMANN, Torald. 'The Crucial Test of Therapeutic Evidence'. *Journal of American Medical Association* 69 (1917): 198–9.

THOMPSON, E. P. *The Making of the English Working Class*. Harmondsworth: Penguin Books, 1968.

TIMPANARO, Sebastiano. *Die Entstehung der Lachmannschen Methode* (Dieter Irmer trans.). Hamburg: Buske Verlag, 1971.

——. *Il lapsus freudiano: Psicoanalisi e filologia testuale*. Firenze: La Nuova Italia, 1975.

——. *La genesi del metodo del Lachmann* (Elio Montanari introd.). Firenze: Le Monnier 2003[1963].

TRAPP, J. B. (ed.). *E. H. Gombrich: A Bibliography*. London: Phaidon Press, 2000.

TREXLER, Richard C. 'Dressing and Undressing Images: An Analytic Sketch' in *Religion in Social Context in Europe and America, 1200–1700*. Tempe: Arizona Center for Medieval and Renaissance Studies, 2002, pp. 374–408.

VISINTIN, Dario. *Michele Soppe benandante*. Santa Maria la Longa (Udine) and Montereale Valcellina (Pordenone): Circolo Culturale Menocchio, 2009.

VOLNEY, Constantin-Francois de Chasseboeuf. *Leçons d'histoire prononcées à l'École normale, en l'an III de la République française*. Paris: J. A. Brosson, third ed. 1826[1799].

WIKIPEDIA. 'Placebo'. *Wikipedia, The Free Encyclopedia*. Available at https://en.wikipedia.org/w/index.php?title=Placebo&oldid=1072376839 (last accessed on 11 March 2022).

Sources

'Civilization and Barbarism' was first published in *Signs Systems Studies* 45(3–4) (2017): 249–62.

'The Soul of Brutes' was first published as 'L'anima dei bruti. Una discussione cinquecentesca' in *Conversazioni per Alberto Gajano* (Carlo Ginzburg and Emanuela Scribano eds) (Pisa: Edizioni ETS, 2005), pp. 163–75.

'Calvino, Manzoni and the Gray Zone' was first published as 'Calvino, Levi et la zone grise', Introduction to Primo Levi, *La zone grise. Entretien avec Anna Bravo et Federico Cereja* (Martin Rueff trans.) (Paris: Payot and Rivages, 2014), pp. 9–26.

'Schema and Bias: A Historian's Reflection on Double-Blind Experiments' was first published as 'Schemi, preconcetti, esperimenti a doppio cieco. Riflessioni di uno storico', *Mefisto* 1(1) (2017): 57–78. Republished in *Occhiacci di legno: Dieci riflessioni sulla distanza* (Macerata: Quodlibet, 2019).

Illustration Credits

The Soul of Brutes

FIGURE 1: Parmigianino, *Self-Portrait with a bitch*. Public-domain image, from Wikimedia Commons.

FIGURE 2: School of Giulio Bonasone, *Portrait of Parmigianino*.

FIGURE 3: Ugo da Carpi, *Diogenes*. Public-domain image, from Wikimedia Commons.

FIGURE 4: Achille Bocchi, *Symbolicarum Quaestionum*. Public-domain image from archive.org

FIGURE 5: Parmigianino's contract 1531 (Santa Maria della Steccata, Parma)

Schema and Bias

FIGURE 1A: Robert Garland, *Chartres Cathedral* (1836). Engraving after a lithograph from B. Winkles, *French Cathedrals* (London, 1837). High-resolution image courtesy Britton-Images.

FIGURE 1B: Present-day photograph of Chartres Cathedral. Public-domain image from Wikimedia Commons.

FIGURE 2: William Hogarth, *Some Principal Inhabitants of the Moon: Royalty, Episcopacy and Law* (1724). Public-domain image, from Wikimedia Commons.

FIGURE 3: Francisco de Goya, *Caprichos No. 52: 'Lo que puede un Sastre!'* Public-domain image, from Wikimedia Commons.

FIGURE 4: Francisco de Goya, Preparatory drawing for *Caprichos No. 52*. Public-domain image, from Wikimedia Commons.